STRANGE
TRADE

THE STORY OF
TWO WOMEN WHO
RISKED EVERYTHING
IN THE INTERNATIONAL
DRUG TRADE

Asale Angel-Ajani

SEAL PRESS

Strange Trade
The Story of Two Women Who Risked Everything in the International Drug Trade

Copyright © 2010 by Asale Angel-Ajani

Published by
Seal Press
A Member of the Perseus Books Group
1700 Fourth Street
Berkeley, California

Library of Congress Cataloging-in-Publication Data

Angel-Ajani, Asale.
  Strange trade : the story of two women who risked everything in the international
drug trade / Asale Angel-Ajani.
      p. cm.
  ISBN 978-1-58005-313-6
  1. Women prisoners--Italy--Rome. 2. Drug traffic--Italy. 3. Rebibbia (Prison :
Rome, Italy) 4. Prisons--Italy. I. Title.
  HV9695.R62R433 2010
  363.45092'245632--dc22

For Alan J. Hanson
and
Mary Johnson

CONTENTS

Prologue: *Cui Bono*

A WHITE MAN, a black man, and an Arab man walked into the room. The beginnings of a bad joke were not lost on me, but I was not sure which was more cringe-inducing: the three men who were approaching my table or the fact that I was about to meet a couple of drug traffickers and an assassin at a fast-food chain called Wimpy's.

I wanted to believe that I didn't want to be here. In fact, for weeks I had tried desperately to act like I didn't want to take part in any of this. I tried feigning illness. I stopped answering my phone. I busily wandered the streets of Rome until I thought I was being followed, and then I hid in my apartment. While I resisted meeting with these men for as long as I could, there was no doubt that this gathering was inevitable. And now, as I watched these men walk toward me, I knew with absolute certainty that the comfortable student life of research and study that I had built in Italy was over.

The three men who were approaching my table worked for one of the largest international drug-smuggling rings operating out Africa, Asia, and Southern Europe. The first man to reach the table was a short, skinny white guy with the palest skin I'd seen in Italy. Luca's short, dark hair was plastered to his forehead with a thick, glossy coat of gel. Behind him was Jojo, a moonfaced Nigerian of medium height, and following Jojo was Hassan, a tall, strikingly handsome Sudanese with black hair.

These were the men who were to be my escorts into the underworld. Seven months ago, I had met their boss in prison, an infamous drug lord known as "the Ugandan." Even though she was behind bars, it was impossible for these men to resist the demands of the Ugandan. I, on the other hand, could have said no. But instead I said yes.

CHAPTER 1.

American Girl, Roman Prison

THE BUS DEPOSITED ME on a street that had no sidewalk. Alone, I walked next to a dusty lot that faced the prison. Weeds tangled themselves up along the edge of the road, until they eventually killed each other off. Their brown, stringy carcasses seemed foreboding. I crossed the street and drifted over to the right, closer to the wall. As I walked, an unforgiving sun sat on my head. Under its weight my body began to rebel; sweat gathered above my lip, on my nose, at my hairline, and under my arms. I paused to take off my jacket. Passing under the guard towers, I felt small but still conspicuous, like a single ant crawling across a plain white surface.

Rebibbia was massive. I stared forward, noting that the prison wall dropped off on the horizon. The gravel was ruining my new boots. I tried to walk more lightly, but I felt myself sinking under the unbearable heat of the sun. Trying to look official on this, my very first day at Rebibbia's women's prison, I had overdressed in an outfit more appropriate for a funeral. The blacks and grays of my shirt, pants, socks, and jacket had the sole purpose of making me sweat. Tension began to shoot up the back of my neck and toward the sides of my face, up near my temples. I wanted to loosen the tight knot taming my habitually unruly hair.

Then I saw what I thought was the entrance to the female prison. There were two big steel doors painted bright blue. The color was cartoonish and too cheery for a place like this. I went up to the doors and saw that there were no doorknobs. I took a few steps back to see if I had missed a sign. There was only a plaque that read REBIBBIA FEMMINILE.

REBIBBIA IS ONE OF ITALY'S prisons. It has held some of the world's most infamous convicts, from Mafia bosses and terrorists to war criminals. Youssef al-Molqi, who was charged with the murder of Leon Klinghoffer during the 1985 hijacking of the *Achille Lauro* cruise ship, and Ali Agca, the would-be assassin of Pope John Paul II, both were incarcerated here. Former Nazi SS captain Erich Priebke and Major Karl Hass spent time in the prison during their highly publicized trial some fifty years after their participation in the 1944 massacre at the Ardeatine caves near Rome.

Rebibbia has also housed some important Italian radicals, the best known among them anarchist Carlo Tesseri, leftist intellectual and former professor Antonio Negri, and, in the female facility, Silvia Baraldini, who was transferred to Rebibbia after spending fourteen years imprisoned in the United States for allegedly assisting in the escape of ex–Black Panther Assata Shakur. In a country with more than sixty thousand inmates, the presence of these and other criminal luminaries confirms Rebibbia's status as the crown jewel of Italy's penitentiaries.

TO VOLUNTARILY ENTER ITALY'S largest prison is not on every American's travel itinerary when she visits Rome, but I'll admit that I am drawn to prisons like a rubberneck is drawn to the scene of a car accident. The reasons for this strange obsession of mine are not complicated—it has everything to do with my childhood. Both of my parents have been incarcerated in some form or fashion: My father was a long-term resident at a federal facility in California from the time I was a baby, and my mother was sent to jail when I was five years old. As a child, I thought of prisons as people-eating machines. It seems only natural, I suppose, that I would have eventually found Rebibbia, at least only to know where it was on the map.

I had first come to Italy when I was in college. I had come alone and without a plan. I had no real interest in Italy or Europe, but I had met loads of people who had fallen in love with the country, the language, or the culture. My first time in Italy, I fell in love with a man. He was fifteen years older than I was, handsome, and terminally ill, and neither one of us spoke the other's language. Doomed to fail, it was brief and melodramatic—the perfect Italian romance.

It wasn't until a few years later, in 1996, when I was in graduate school studying anthropology at Stanford University and needed a subject for my dissertation research, that Italy came to mind as a good place to study race and identity. I had thought about the United States, France, and even a few countries in Africa. I am not sure what finally brought my attention to Italy—maybe I thought it would be easy, since I had already spent some time there. Also, I knew slightly more Italian than I did French, which is to say that I could order a sandwich to go with my espresso.

But before trotting off to do fieldwork—a standard tour of duty for any anthropologist—I spent years boning up on all things vaguely related to the subject of my research on race and immigration in Italy. I took language classes and spent even more time in Italy. I did all of this with little enthusiasm. Then I received a long-distance call from Naples, the city where I had proposed to do my study. I remember that I was sitting in my nearly empty apartment, a few days before my planned departure, when the telephone rang. It was my friend Rahim. He was breathless and agitated, shouting, "Call me back! Call me back! I don't have money for this." Rahim was a Moroccan student who was forever on the verge of overstaying his Italian visa. He was even more broke than I was, so I knew that his phone call was more than a distraction for him.

It turned out that the police had taken Nellie, a Zambian woman, into custody. No one from the immigrants' rights group that I worked with in Naples knew where she was, but Rome was high on the list of possibilities. I gamely offered my services to help find her because Nellie was a friend who had rescued me once, a few years earlier, and I owed her.

Nellie and I met on an overnight train from Paris to Rome. I was a typical backpacker travelling on a tight budget and hadn't realized that my cheap ticket did not cover a ride on the couchette. Nellie watched as the train conductor yelled at me in French and Italian and English. I was given a fine and told that I was going to be kicked off the train at the next stop at four o'clock in the morning someplace in Southern France. I remember how shocked I was when she reached into her wallet and paid my nearly $100 penalty and then politely told the conductor in impeccable French to leave me alone. Though we parted ways in Rome, me to see the sights and her to her life in Naples, we had remained in contact ever since.

As soon as I got off the phone with Rahim, I made two phone calls: to my friend Stefano, the only person I knew who lived in Rome, and to Alitalia Airlines.

A few weeks later, when I was standing in front of the massive steel doors that separated the outside world from those detained inside Italy's most notorious prison, even I was surprised by the turn of events. As I prepared to enter Rebibbia, my ingrained wisdom about how things work took over. The bureaucratic aspect of prison is not, for me, mysterious: identification, a calmly stated purpose, a small vacant smile— these often helped to open gates. But what I was not prepared for was a distant yet familiar feeling of doubt that had been persistent for most of my youth. Experience had taught me that prisons are the containers of all that haunts and menaces human beings. There is hardly a more depressing place than one designated for people who have failed at life.

When I stood outside the walls of Rebibbia for the first time, I asked myself: *Do I really want to walk into all of this all over again?* I looked up at the guard tower; it was empty. As my eyes scanned along the prison wall, twenty feet ahead I noticed a small window that looked like a ticket booth. I walked on and reached the window. Nothing. Rebibbia was starting to feel like a ghost town. I just needed to get in. I had an appointment and I was already late. Somebody must be expecting me, I reasoned.

I walked back over to the two large doors and was preparing to knock, when I saw a white button. I pressed it. I fanned myself with my hands. I was nervous. I was swaying slightly, trying to make time move faster. I was just about to push the buzzer again, when I heard the shuffling of footsteps behind the door. With a sharp *click,* one side of the large doors opened. A guard wearing a uniform in various shades of blue stuck his head out.

"What do you want?" he asked gruffly in Italian. He was a big man in his mid-fifties.

"I have a meeting with the director." I hated that I sounded so tentative when I spoke Italian.

The guard looked me over from head to toe and gestured with a stiff jerk of his head. "Go to the window." The steel door clanged shut.

I walked over to the window. He sat inside the booth.

"Documents?" he asked.

I handed him everything I needed and then some to establish a credible alibi for wanting to enter the prison: my passport, old student identification cards, proof of my address in Rome, and a fax from the minister of justice giving my visit official approval.

He grabbed the passport and pushed the rest of the paperwork back in my direction. I watched as he picked up the phone and dialed what I assumed was the office of the director.

He repeated different, mangled versions of my name several times to the person on the other end of the phone, who, I could only imagine, kept asking, "What? Who?" Finally, the two of them must have decided it didn't matter. The guard looked at me and said, "Go back to the door."

I waited for a moment, thinking that he would give me back my passport. He stood up with it in his hand and walked out of the window frame.

I quickly walked back over to the steel door. He was waiting for me. He opened it just enough that I could squeeze past him. I stepped inside a large concrete garage. This was where they brought the prisoners through.

To the left was another booth. The guard went inside to a desk and passed a large book across the counter that separated us. "Sign your name here and the date here," he said, pointing firmly to two separate columns.

"Go over there," he then ordered, pointing to a metal detector that I hadn't noticed when I'd first walked in. He held up my passport. "I will keep this until you return."

I hesitated. In my mind flashed all of the warning sections in those travel books I had read back in the States. The words varied in their degree of paranoia, but the gist was always the same: Never let your passport out of your sight. Carry it with you at all times. Since I had started traveling, I had been led to believe that my American passport was certainly as valuable as, if not more so than, my cash. My eyes lingered on the gold eagle embossed on the blue cover. The guard flapped the passport back and forth twice. *Come in or stay out,* his gesture seemed to say.

Reluctantly, I walked over to the metal detector. It looked like the ones they had in the banks in Naples. It was a glass cage. I walked through one glass door and waited until a guard, a lanky young man who seemed to appear from out of nowhere, motioned me through to the other side.

"Take her to the office," the older guard shouted to him.

The young guard didn't say anything. He went through the door that connected the garage to the prison's inner sanctum. The second I crossed over the threshold, I noticed how the sky seemed bluer. The leaves on the trees rustled as a breeze moved calmly between them. I ambled behind the guard as we walked up a paved semicircular incline lined with trees, bushes, and flowering plants.

Just as we neared the top of the hill, I could see a building with bars on the windows off to my right, sitting amid thick green grass. Oddly, there was something serene about it. In some of the barred windows, brightly printed African fabric billowed, giving life to the breeze. There was a big tree in the foreground with a picnic bench in the shade underneath it. Directly ahead of me, two huge flowering bushes flanked another building. This was where the administrative offices were.

I lingered at the edge of the bushes, trying to get a glimpse of the landscape behind them. I couldn't see anything, but I imagined that the rest of the prison was unfurled in an array of bunkers at the foot of this little hill. And I was certain that it wasn't nearly as bucolic as this area.

Inside the administrative building, the walls were painted a garish yellow-orange. The floor was tiled in a similar color but was more tan than yellow. The impossibly high ceiling amplified every toe tap. Sound reverberated throughout the entire length of the corridor.

The guard walked into a large office. "Where's Maria?" he asked a dark-haired woman sitting on top of her desk, talking to a short, balding prison guard.

"Oh, is this the American?" She and the guard looked at me skeptically. I was clearly not what they had been expecting.

"I don't know. I was told to bring her here."

Annoyed at the way they spoke about me as if I weren't there, I chimed in with too much authority. "Yes, I am the American. I have an appointment with the director. Is this her office?"

They stared at me, dumbfounded. It was as if I had just spoken to them in pig Latin and they were trying to decipher my message. But this was a line I had rehearsed over and over again in Italian. I had said it perfectly. They looked at each other, trying to figure out who should answer first.

The dark-haired woman spoke. "Doctor Zainaghi is not in today."

"What?" I asked, surprised. *That can't be true,* I thought to myself. *My meeting was confirmed just yesterday.*

"You are the one who is here to conduct interviews, correct?" A female voice came from behind me. This was obviously the Maria whom I was supposed to meet.

Maria approached me and said, "I read your fax. We have set everything up for you."

"Will I get to speak to the director?" I asked. "I was supposed to meet with her today."

"Don't worry about that. Please, come with me." She led me out the door, back into the gaudy hallway. I didn't have to walk far to see that there had been a huge mistake.

Against the wall stood about thirty-five African women. I quickly scanned their faces and was filled with disappointment when I saw that Nellie was not among them. Maria stopped and stood in the front of the line and asked me, "How long will this take?"

I stared down the row of women. Some had faces that were shiny with sweat; some were short, others tall. Some of them looked bored, others smiled, openly amused. I was overwhelmed by their sheer humanity. Did she think I was going to interview all of these people at once? Silently but frantically, I began to pull my Italian vocabulary together. "I would like to speak to each of the women privately, one at a time. Is there a room that I can use?" I wasn't sure if I had been delicate with my tone. My voice rattled at too high a pitch and echoed off the ceiling. I thought I sounded hysterical.

"You want to interview them one at a time?" Her eyes narrowed. "I am not sure we can do that."

I looked at the women. They looked back at me, mostly with curiosity. One woman quickly smiled politely and then hid her eyes. She was older than the others. She had high cheekbones. Her eyes were perfectly shaped almonds that seemed gently placed in her thin and angular face. Something about her manner seemed to silently encourage me.

"But I would like to speak to all of the women," I repeated, turning back to Maria. "Isn't there some way I can speak to some women today, the ones who want to talk to me, and then come back tomorrow and the day after so that I can speak to everyone?" I knew that prisons are institutions that do not generally strive for transparency. And I was a person from the outside, a foreigner no less, who had the privilege of getting past the visiting room. Looking at the women she'd hand selected for me to interview, I sensed that Maria wanted to control the process as much as she could.

Maria looked at me skeptically. "I don't know. Do you have permission to come back and forth to do interviews?"

I panicked. I wasn't sure if I had made that clear in my request letter to the minister of justice. Even if I had, I wasn't certain that the minister had made it clear to the prison that I had permission to conduct multiple interviews.

"Uh, I-I am certain that I do," I stammered.

"Okay, we'll see. I will bring some women to you." A pack of cigarettes and a lighter appeared magically in her hands. She walked toward the exit. "Meet me in the office. The guard will show you the way."

I took one last look at the women, who stayed unmoving against the wall, and then at the guard, who had walked ahead of me by several paces. Besides the *educatora,* or social worker, Maria, who had just left me so she could go have a smoke, I knew of no one else that I could ask about Nellie. But looking at the faces of the thirty-five women and seeing their hope, their fear, their disgust, their anger, their curiosity, their kindness, I knew that I had signed on for something bigger than finding Nellie. I had stumbled into a world where these women were but shadows of themselves. And if there were thirty-five of these women standing out here, then there were more than thirty-five African women in other parts of the prison that I was not seeing.

What I didn't know then was that none of them would be Nellie. And by the time I heard word from her several months later, she was living safely with her sister in Paris. It was just as well because once I was inside Rebibbia, I found it very difficult to just up and leave.

CHAPTER 2.
Urbi et Orbi

FALL HIT THE CITY suddenly. It came like the morning when someone wakes up, looks in the mirror, and sees the first signs of aging. As with any grim reaper worth its salt, autumn brought a different kind of death to Rome. Gone were the tourist groups who took up entire street corners and sidewalks, following young women holding up a plastic flower or an umbrella, straining to hear high-pitched and nasal descriptions of this renowned street or that famous relic. Gone was the outdoor seating in front of restaurants and cafés. Gone were the sunny days, the slow walks in the park, and the boarded-up shops with signs saying CLOSED. ENJOY YOUR HOLIDAY. Instead, there was urgency in the city as old ladies knocked each other over to grab seats on crowded buses and middle-aged women hurried down busy streets with too many shopping bags. Men in suit jackets walked at a brisk pace to get around loud, meandering schoolchildren and risked their lives by hopping into the street and into the path of screeching, bleating scooters.

I watched the season take hold of Rome from an uncomfortable plastic seat on bus 319 as I headed home from a long day at the prison. I had been conducting interviews at Rebibbia for nearly three months. After my first day at Rebibbia, where I interviewed just a handful of the thirty-five women that Maria had introduced me too, I knew that I would not be going back to go to Naples to do my research. After talking to incarcerated women from all over Africa about their problems and issues they faced both within and outside of prison, their concerns seemed far more immediate than the general investigation of the meaning of race and identity in Italy. Since I had waited nearly a month for the minister of justice to reply to my initial request, I called their offices to confirm that I could use their permission to go back to Rebibbia as long as the prison administrators let me. It was a first for them: an American woman wanting to go inside the prison only to speak to African convicts? No one knew what to make of me.

TODAY, I HAD FINALLY met an infamous inmate called simply "the Ugandan." Not long after I had first arrived at Rebibbia, I had started hearing stories about this person, and within weeks these tales had taken on an almost mythical quality. In the men's prison, I heard about how the Ugandan led a paramilitary force of criminals, and that for inspiration the Ugandan read aloud from the ancient Chinese military manual "The Art of War." In the women's prison, I learned that from Paris to the Kenyan bush, the Ugandan knew the whereabouts of every employee's dearest loved one at all times, and used this information as an insurance policy to protect against theft or other forms of betrayal. The gossip was that the Ugandan lived in vast luxury, worked with the Mafia, and had police, customs, and other government officials on payroll. The more outlandish rumors were that the Ugandan drank some kind of elixir each day to penetrate thoughts or shield bullets (depending on the narrator), or that the Ugandan could enter a room like a zephyr and kill people as they slept.

At first, I found the tales of the Ugandan curious but mostly absurd, so I didn't pursue the story. Then I met her. Her name was Pauline Zeno. I had seen her around the prison before. She seemed to be one of the few inmates who could roam freely—from her cellblock to the main administrative offices, where I sat conducting interviews. It was easy to notice her. Aside from Pauline's obviously privileged status (virtually no inmates except those on official business came up to the administrative offices), she was exceedingly gregarious, though not in any way solicitous. She would often enter the office with a boisterous "hello" to no one in particular.

I watched from my vantage point on the sidelines, and though Pauline didn't even look in my direction, I still found her charming. I was not alone in my opinion, as she could get everyone from the guards to the office workers laughing and smiling. She had mass appeal, though she was rather ordinary. Pauline was of medium height and had a thick, muscular body. Though I figured out that she was about forty-four years old when we met, Pauline could have been anywhere between thirty and fifty-five. She always seemed to wear the same pair of light-yellow sweatpants, white running shoes, and a white T-shirt. She wore her hair in thin braids that went past her shoulders. She wasn't especially pretty, but she did have nice wide eyes and an easy smile.

When she sat down for our first interview, she was carrying a large manila envelope and two books. I immediately asked her what she was reading: *Moby Dick.* She held it up for me. "It's a favorite. I read it again and again." I was intrigued but skeptical. She picked up the other book, a slim volume. It was Euripides' play *Medea.* "I was in the production that they did here last year, but I was only in the chorus. Next time, I intend to play the lead, Medea," she told me without a trace of humility. "Now, do you mind if we get on with this interview?"

Pauline started by telling me where I lived. "Via Rendano." She took a piece of paper out of her envelope and slid it across the table to me. It listed the first names of nearly all the men and women whom I had spoken with in the prison. "Relax," she said as I looked at her and the list with a mix of confusion and worry.

"You have been here a couple of months now, right? Pauline asked in a way that told me that she knew, perhaps better than I did, exactly how long I had been working in

Rebibbia. "You take a special interest in all of these people," she said, pointing to her list, "it's only smart for someone to ask why. So I wanted to know if you worked for the police." She didn't react to my shaking head. "I understand that you have an obligation to me, correct?"

"What do you mean?" I asked. I was getting nervous and a little scared.

"Well, you are a professional, are you not?" I felt self-conscious and launched into my well-practiced speech about my responsibility to protect her identity. She waved her hand, indicating for me to stop.

"I am not worried," she said with a mischievous smile. "I have heard your Italian."

WHEN I FIRST STARTED speaking with women in Rebibbia who'd been caught smuggling drugs, I, like most people, thought I knew the basic details of their day-to-day reality. They were women who had fallen on hard times or women who had been coerced by the men in their lives. And yes, I felt sympathy for them, but they were somewhat alien to me, despite the fact that my own mother had shared their experience. But the more I talked with people, not just in Italy but elsewhere in the world, the more I began to meet women who were a lot like me. These women were in their late twenties or thirties, some were college educated and were on specific career paths, and they all had high ambitions. They were smart women. They were savvy about the world and had a clear sense of right and wrong. Yet something had happened in their lives that had caused them to swallow fistfuls of heroin or lug suitcases full of drugs around the globe.

As much as I wanted to know why women were among the fastest-growing population in narcotrafficking, I was even more curious about women like Pauline—who didn't see drug smuggling as merely a quick, if dangerous, way to get out of debt, but who had jumped headfirst into this world as a career move.

From a distance, Pauline certainly did not fit the image that I had created of the Ugandan. The Ugandan seemed like a character Hollywood would dream up. The Ugandan was a feared, illusive, wealthy, and respected bad guy, the perfect villain. In the movies the Ugandan would be a man, not a woman, and certainly not a seemingly ordinary wife and mother, like Pauline was. I didn't think it was possible to meet a woman who profited off the use of other women to transport drugs back and forth over borders. But here she was, the leader of one of the most efficient and expansive drug rings in Africa and Europe. Pauline, the Ugandan, was unique, but certainly she was not alone.

GLOBALLY, DRUG SMUGGLING IS the most profitable of all illegal trades. It is at least a $500-billion-a-year industry (a sum that is on par with the U.S. Department of Defense's annual budget for the fiscal years 2004–2009). No other industry, legal or illegal, can claim the returns that drug smuggling can.

Weak governments, terrorists, warmongers, and even legitimate businesses benefit from illicit drug trading.

Drug cartels both large and small have been outsmarting law enforcement for years with increasingly sophisticated techniques for transporting narcotics. After large shipments are brought into Africa via boats, planes, trucks, and even submarines, many methods are used to break up large parcels of drugs for European consumption. One of the West African traffickers' preferred approaches to getting drugs across borders is the use of human smugglers—known as "body packers," "swallowers," or "mules." These days, many drug smugglers are women, because they're more likely to go unnoticed by authorities.

Drug lords like Pauline find women easy to control through intimidation—and besides, most women who traffic need money desperately. Though I would later learn that Pauline had other methods of transporting drugs, I knew that many traffickers send two to twenty female smugglers on a single flight, thus increasing their odds of maximizing profits. It's a good strategy. Given the 1.5 billion–plus travelers in the air worldwide per year, plus the fact that a single courier can swallow up to $300,000 worth of premium heroin (which can be street-ready within hours), drug cartels are willing to risk exposure for such high returns.

Body packers aren't like street dealers, waiting for addicts to purchase their goods. And these women are not like the bosses at the helm of the trafficking rings. Swallowers are like contract employees—they do a few runs and then disappear into society's fold. That's why the fastest way to learn about these women is to go to the prisons, where the numbers of female inmates are swelling rapidly, largely due to drug charges.

Italy has experienced some of the highest rates of drug smuggling in all of Europe; 55 percent of the female prisoners are foreigners and over half of them were arrested for smuggling drugs through Italy for the European market. I knew I was lucky to arrive at Rebibbia during a time when not only were countless women from all over the world being caught smuggling drugs, but also, by some strange fluke, one of their bosses was right there with them.

THE EVENING AFTER I met Pauline, I pondered her demeanor and her self-possession. She was so unlike the other women I'd met at Rebibbia so far. It wasn't just because she was the Ugandan; it was because of the way that she had expertly controlled every moment of our interaction. I'd heard enough about her to know that this skill was part of her personality. She was smart; after all, she had brought photos and other props to illustrate her stories. She had told me exactly what she wanted to without seeming like she was hiding anything. What I did not yet understand was why she would have wanted to talk to me in the first place. She didn't seem to have the need for visitors, unlike some of the other women I met.

I have to admit that I was flattered that she'd spoken with me. But still, I was worried. I began wondering how, exactly, she had gotten my address, how she knew who else

I'd spoken with? During our interview, I had been just scared enough to not ask her myself. Had she asked prison officials? She seemed to have some friends among them. Was she having me followed? It was possible. Walking home from my bus stop, I looked into the windows of passing cars; paranoia settled in. I remembered a papal phrase that Pauline had used hours earlier to describe the reach of her business: *urbi et orbi,* "to the city of Rome and to the world."

CHAPTER 3.
The Place to Be

REBIBBIA IS A SPRAWLING prison perched on the edge of Rome, with clandestine entrances, hidden rooms, bunkers, and sealed-off wards. I took the metro there nearly every morning; from Stazione Termini, Rome's transportation mecca, I jostled my way on the train that would carry me twenty-five minutes to the very end of the line. With each stop, the crowd thinned, leaving a motley crew of rough-looking Italians and bleary-eyed immigrants from India, the Philippines, Senegal, Albania, and Ecuador. During my commute, I would think about my interviews from the day before. As I made my way out of the subway, I would start preparing myself mentally to spend the day in a room with stagnant air and little sunlight.

I had grown used to the facility's appearance, and understood the cadence of the place. I might have been in Rome, but Rebibbia was similar to any prison, anywhere in the world. I had grown used to seeing the families of the accused and convicted corralled into a small waiting room, almost like a hallway, before visiting hours began. After a quick inspection of their handbags and a pass through the metal detector, they were ushered into a large room with hard plastic chairs. In those chairs they fidgeted impatiently, waiting for their loved ones to be called.

It isn't difficult to see who among the visitors has woven the thick, impenetrable wire of prison into their lives. Mostly older women, they are the ones with Teflon skin and busyness in their eyes, though, oddly, their bodies are relaxed. They even smile and ask the guards about their children, wives, or mothers. Meanwhile, those who are new to the ritual or visit infrequently stand uncomfortably in line and have a habit of glancing over their shoulders. They are the ones who cannot hide their sadness or their shame when their loved ones walk into the room.

ONCE INSIDE REBIBBIA, AFTER all the activity of going through metal detectors and depositing my bag in a locker or leaving it with the on-duty officer, followed by a brief interview with a guard who confirmed my identity and made certain that I had no weapons, camera, or recording equipment, I was either taken to an interview room normally used by attorneys or given a desk in a large office where the social workers sat. I liked the large office. It was usually empty, so

I could have privacy, and it was closer to the administrative heart of the prison, so the women who chose to come and talk to me could be close to their wards, jobs, or classes.

The other room, the interview room, was depressing and tiny and far off the beaten path of anyone's daily routine, and there was far more scrutiny there, since it was so far from the center of the prison. Signing in and out, plus frequent interruptions by security-minded guards, was routine.

On the day that I met Mary, I was kept waiting in such a room for two hours. I was convinced that I had been forgotten, but I didn't get up to ask the guard again what was taking so long. Instead, I took in the sounds of the prison. The noise was constant. Echoes bumped into each other, tumbled, and then seemed to bounce back upward again. Mostly, it sounded like the clanging of steel, but with softer, distant notes. Even when I could dissect a voice out from all the clattering or catch a patch of words, it was useless—nothing was legible.

I took in the room. The table was a chipped and dulled Formica top. The two chairs were wooden, uncomfortable. I had never been in an interrogation room before, but if I had ever had to imagine one, it would have looked like this. The ceiling was almost too high. The hanging fluorescent light took up most of the airspace above; I was thankful that it was turned off. But what I was really looking for were signs of a camera.

Knowing that I was being watched by some faceless power caused me to be still. Sudden movements can bring too much attention, draw lazy eyes to your part of the prison, wake half-sleeping guards, invite inquiry. I worried that if I openly looked around too much, it might appear as if I were plotting a prison break.

Why is it taking so long? I wondered for what seemed to be the hundredth time. I put my hands on the table in plain view, next to the only things I was allowed to bring in with me: a notepad and a pen. I turned my body in the chair to face the door. I waited.

THE DAY BEFORE, TANIA, a social worker at Rebibbia, came up to me as I was leaving for the day.

"There you are!" she said in a flush of excitement. "I was hoping I would see you. Come have a coffee with me." Tania was the only prison official with whom I spoke English, though I was speaking mostly English with the women I interviewed—since many of them were from anglophone Africa.

"Oh?" I asked. I liked Tania; she seemed different from the other social workers. She was always smiling, which was unusual to see during an average day in the prison. She wore jeans, driving loafers, and a crisp button-up shirt rolled up over her jewel-laden wrists nearly every day, presenting the impression that she had somehow taken a wrong turn out of Rome on her way to her country estate.

"Don't just stand there, *bella,* come." I followed her out of the office toward a part of the prison that I had never seen before. The canteen was teeming with prison staffers, standing around drinking espresso and smoking cigarettes. After we ordered our coffee, I waited for Tania to lead the way to one of the empty tables scattered around. Instead, she moved closer toward the door, away from the busy barista.

"There's a woman I want you to meet," she said, her smile gone. "I'm not going to tell you much about her, but I will say that she has had quite a life." She leaned in closer to me to say, "Her name is Mary. Some people here don't like her. They think she's difficult, but I like her very much."

I nodded my head, preoccupied by the gold charms jangling on her bracelets. I forced myself to look up at her when she spoke. Tania was a tall woman with thick black hair that fell in messy waves to her shoulders. Her nose took over most of her face. Long and squared at the tip, it pulled her cheekbones in as she spoke.

"Why do you want me to meet her?" I wasn't sure if this woman was an inmate or a co-worker.

Tania smiled and shrugged her shoulders. "Because you should know her. That's all. And she has agreed to talk to you."

Since Tania had set up my interview with Mary, I thought perhaps we had mixed up our meeting time. But suddenly, I heard the sound of the guard getting up from his chair to open the gate that the inmates came through. And then she appeared. Standing in the doorway was a large woman, as tall as she was wide. Tania had told me that Mary was thirty-six years old, about ten years older then me at the time, and I immediately felt each one of the years between us.

"Let's get this over with," she said. "I have somewhere to be." Mary began abruptly, and motioned for me to get out my pen and paper. She had been through this before, she was letting me know, doing interviews with people who pass through the prison. I listened to Mary roll out her life story in a well-rehearsed script.

"You are not writing," she said when she noticed that I'd set down my pen.

"No," I said, aware that I was looking for a way to show Mary that I knew she was playing a role, presumably one she put on for prison officials and their guests. "I really just wanted to meet you. Besides, you have some place to be and, if it is okay with you, I would like to come back when you have more time to talk."

Mary looked at me, trying to determine if I had any tricks up my sleeve. Finally she said, "Really, you are coming back?"

I nodded. "Tomorrow or the next day or whenever is best for you."

"And these people will let you come when you like?" Mary laughed when I nodded again.

"Okay . . . " Mary motioned at me, searching for my name.

"Asale," I offered.

"Okay, Asale, if you can get these people to let you back in here, then we can talk. Right now I am working, so if you want some of my time you will have to come in the afternoons."

"Alright, so I will come in the afternoon. Tomorrow." We were both smiling when she stood up from the table.

When she got to the door she said, "And see if you can't meet me a little closer to the office. This building is too far to walk to. No one wants to come out here."

Now I laughed along with Mary—her request fell outside of my limited power in the prison and we both knew it. "See you tomorrow," I called after her. She held up her crossed fingers without turning to look back at me.

I gathered up my things and set off to find Tania. I was determined to meet with Mary the following day and move our interview closer to the central office if I could arrange it. I was happy that I'd met Mary. I had a sense that over time, we could become good friends.

CHAPTER 4.
Mary and James

IT WAS 1990, AT the start of West Africa's rainy season. James had come home quiet and short-tempered. Mary didn't think much of his mood; she figured he was having a problem at his office. The war had strangled any business that was not about guns or the timber or rubber that were used to buy guns, but her husband went to work daily just to keep up his routine. It was difficult and they were going without, but Mary prided herself on how normal their lives were: James leaving for his office daily, regular mealtimes for the children, their scheduled music lessons. But by the time she put his dinner in front of him, she could see he was agitated.

In their fourteen years of marriage, he had never been the brooding type. "Is it work?" she asked.

His eyes were deep brown. She noticed that they were bloodshot. "We'll discuss it later." He picked up his fork and began eating.

AFTER THE DINNER PLATES were cleared and the children asleep, Mary waited for James in the night shadows of their bedroom. It was nearly midnight by the time she heard a light tap and then the door opening. Mary reached over and turned on a small lamp near the bed.

"No. Please." James held his hand up to his face to shield his eyes. Mary said nothing and quickly clicked off the light.

James settled into the chair by the side of the bed. "They were at the office today, waiting for me. I managed to get rid of them, but for how long?"

"Who was it?" Mary asked.

"Does it matter?" His words prickled with anxiety. The warlord Charles Taylor had sent his men. They did not yet control the capital, but it seemed possible that they could in a matter of days. Taylor, an upper-class Liberian, had launched his coup from the north of the Ivory Coast and had taken nearly six months to reach Monrovia. He and his small band of Libyan-trained rebels were leading a ferocious battle to rid Liberia of president Samuel Doe, scorching, fleecing, beating, or killing anyone or anything that they perceived to be in their way.

"Can you give them money?" Mary's eyes fished around in the darkness.

"Money?" James hissed, "Mary, I don't have enough money to keep them away—why can't you understand? This time they ask, next time they take. They have guns. I have a family. Surely you see that we are not safe?"

Mary let his words hang in the silence before she sat up on the bed. She could smell him, Palmolive soap mixed with onions and sweat. It was a smell that used to comfort her. James leaned in close and turned on the light again. They both blinked their eyes, startled by its brightness.

"We are leaving, then?" Mary could not imagine abandoning their home in Monrovia, Liberia's capital city. She was nervous.

James leaned forward in his chair. "We need to head east. I think we have a better chance once we reach Tapeta." They were going to travel to James's family's home.

Mary nodded. Liberia is a small country, about the size of the state of Tennessee. It is divided up into counties; Tapeta is in the northeastern county of Nimba. From there, they would try to make it across the border to the Ivory Coast.

Mary did not look at her husband's clasped hands. Her eyes moved up his arm to the top of his head. She noticed that his circle of thinning hair was getting larger.

"Yes. Fine." She had considered the possibility that her family would be a target once the war's poverty reached the city. James was a successful engineer; though they were not rich, they had enough money so that when the rest of Monrovia's population ran out of it, they would look upon her house— behind a thick cement wall, with guards and dogs—and begin to wonder what her family was trying to protect.

She scanned their bedroom. They lived modestly. Their relative wealth was not the only thing that they were trying to keep safe. Yes, it was their children, but it was more than that. It was their way of life, the normalcy of it. Why had they jeopardized this by staying in Liberia so long? she wondered.

CHAPTER 5.

The Martyr and the Murderess

A COUPLE WEEKS LATER was the first time I witnessed an encounter between the martyr and the murderess. I was interviewing Pauline when Mary's body filled the doorway, causing Pauline to stop talking and quickly stand up. The locking of their eyes seemed to cut any sound from the small interview room, making distant the hollow noise of the prison. Since the women stared at each other with the obvious disgust of two people with a long and painful history, I didn't bother to introduce them. Instead, I waited to see who would speak first. But Pauline pushed silently past Mary, going out into the hallway. As she did, Mary's large body teetered slightly and then steadied itself against the doorframe. Mary looked at me with dull black eyes, making her revulsion clear by loudly sucking her teeth. It was a quick, angry sound.

Pauline snorted a laugh. She wanted to appear relaxed, but I could see that she was rigid with tension, one fist clenched tightly by her side. Despite their hatred of each other, Pauline seemed too proud to acknowledge the fact openly.

Mary waited for Pauline to turn down the hall and out of eyesight before she spoke.

"What are you doing speaking to her? You know nothing about her. I am telling you, she is a dangerous person. You have to stay away from her." Mary was pacing the floor. "Listen to me. I know what I am talking about. I have talked to the other girls—even some of the girls that work for her. Stay away, Asale. She is the devil, I promise you."

I was grateful that Mary was concerned for me, but also surprised. We had had a few meetings together, and though she seemed maternal, I didn't have enough of a sense of her to know if that's just how she was, or whether she felt a deeper kinship with me. I did know, however, that I was not going to stop talking to Pauline just yet. So I tried to reassure her: "Please don't worry about me. I'll be fine. Really. I know what I'm doing. Besides, I'm just interviewing her, and we talk about pretty much the same things you and I talk about."

This time Mary laughed. "Don't trust her. If you do, you are a fool, like the rest of these people." She went on to tell me that she had "evidence" and "proof" and that she was not a "chatty" woman, so I really needed to heed her warning. "Talk to the others. They will tell you."

I nodded my head slowly, letting her know that I understood. "Did she ever do anything to you? You don't seem to like each other very much."

Mary thought for a while about how to answer this. "Pauline hates me because I am not afraid of her and never will be. I hate her because I have seen what she has done to people. She has made young girls into slaves, selling their bodies, turning them to drugs. She does this to her own kind, to girls that could be her daughters—all for money. So if she thinks she can get something from you, she is going to try. Don't think that you are above all that just because you are sitting on the opposite side of this table."

"Okay, okay," I said, trying to stop her from saying any more. "I will talk to some of the women—just give me their names, and I will see if I can set up an interview." Mary didn't waste any time. She wrote out three names, telling me to be discreet when I called them down for an interview and to wait a couple of weeks before speaking to them. I listened with only half my attention, because I was too busy weighing Mary's warning against what I knew about Pauline. Yes, her reputation was, to put it mildly, pretty bad, but I had not seen any open signs of the violence or danger that people spoke about. True, I was a little nervous around her, and this was justified— the woman had had me followed, after all—but she had also been up front about that.

Maybe I *was* a fool, as Mary called me, but I felt that Pauline and I had a tacit agreement—a professional understanding, if you will, that provided both of us with some protection. She could speak to me openly about who she was without having to fear reprisal, and I could . . . what? I stumbled around, thinking about what my status as a researcher protected me from. I was hard pressed to come up with anything other than a couple of lessons that I had learned in a class I had taken on how to be a researcher. In my mind, I could hear one word from the class being repeated: "privilege." Right, I remembered—I had my privileged background: my U.S. passport, my round-trip ticket out of here, my $200 worth of travelers' checks stuffed in the side pocket of my suitcase at the bottom of my wardrobe. I could walk away. Somehow, though, when I took the list from Mary, my privilege seemed like cold comfort.

CHAPTER 6.
A Year Like Any Other

AT THE START OF the war, everyone who could flee did. But not them. Mary and James had waved off the concerns of their friends and family, scoffed at offers to take the children to safer countries. Now she and James sat with the weight of their ignorance, their arrogance.

It was hard to ignore the realities of the fighting. Mary had kept it out of her home as much as she could. They hired extra guards and made the children stay indoors. They bought more batteries, even used car batteries, when the electricity went out. They did not allow the children to listen to the radio. Mary tried to pretend that everything was fine. But still the war licked at the edges of their lives. When the burst from a gun battle rang out too close to their home, Mary shut the window as if she were keeping out the noise from a nearby party. When sending the children to school became too dangerous, she told them that their school had closed for special holidays.

Mary could not delude herself forever, though—the news was grim. The entire country was held hostage by a war between three factions. Each of the armed groups started with an ideological position, although Mary could no longer recall what those positions were.

The war officially began on Christmas Eve in 1989, when Charles Taylor vowed to bring down the president, Samuel Doe. Doe, a high school–educated master sergeant of the small Krahn tribe, had come to power through his own bloody coup d'état nine years prior to Taylor's arrival. Doe was a short, dark-skinned man with thick glasses and eyes that betrayed his insecurity. He proclaimed that he was for all Liberians, not just the elite-minority Americo-Liberians, the descendants of the freed American slaves who had founded and ruled Liberia since the nineteenth century.

Once in power, Doe, working along ethnic lines and playing with minor tensions between groups, filled the national military, the Armed Forces of Liberia (AFL) and his cabinet with Krahn and Mandingo tribal members, ousting members who seemed to be less sympathetic. When soldiers from the AFL started brutalizing people, especially from the Mano and Gio tribes, hatred for Doe specifically and for the Krahn and the Mandingo generally began to fester.

By the time Charles Taylor, a Gola and Americo-Liberian ethnic mix and a corrupt government official under

Doe, launched his attack, his rebel troops, the National Patriotic Forces of Liberia (NPFL), swelled with eager volunteers. Mary did not like Doe either. She thought he was an uneducated, dangerous, petty, and power-hungry man who was prone to flattery—nothing better than a country bumpkin in her eyes.

On the other hand, she thought Charles Taylor was a true statesman. He was charismatic, well traveled, American-educated, and smart. But Taylor, a light-skinned man with freckles and a habit of speaking about himself in the third person, was also unscrupulous. He was greedy, arrogant, and a liar. Mary knew that Taylor was just as brutal as Doe; in fact, Taylor was even more brutal and more bloodthirsty than Doe, along with his former soldier Prince Yormie Johnson, the leader of the small splinter group, the Independent National Patriotic Forces of Liberia (INPFL). Large and imposing, with fleshy cheeks, Johnson was himself a maniacal killer, inclined to mindless brutality even against his closest friends. He loved gospel music and often sang church songs over the bodies of his victims.

She had put her faith in the city and the national army to protect them. Though she thought little of President Doe, he was the country's leader. During his reign, he had the support of nearly every government in the world. He had even met with U.S. president Ronald Reagan. Surely, Mary thought, no one would stand for a few armed men to take over all of Liberia.

In the years before the war, the atmosphere in Monrovia had been cautiously jubilant. Though Doe was in power and his military was feared, it was a time when many Liberians lived in acquiescence. As the only West African country founded by former American slaves, Liberia enjoyed an almost filial relationship with the United States. This relationship was an insurance policy. For Mary, as for most Liberians, it created a sense of security, though when the U.S. government turned the other cheek after Doe's 1980 coup and did not send aid in the mounting civil war, it was clear that this alliance had failed them.

FOR A LONG TIME, Mary knew her family had to leave Monrovia, which was slowly being taken over by roving gangs of boy soldiers. Drunk and high on drugs, these boys were like the hand grenades they wore on their bodies, just one pin short of exploding.

A second visit from Taylor's men was the writing on the wall. Mary would learn that James had given them money— enough to pay them not to kill him. James knew that it was only a matter of time, perhaps even just few days, before they returned. So, a few hours after he told Mary that the rebels had come to his office, the family gathered just before dawn and drove out of the city.

They left Monrovia as softly as the morning crept in to begin a new day. The place was crawling with displaced people from the countryside, scouring the streets in search of food and clean water. As they departed, Mary looked past the rusty cars and buildings teeming with people seeking shelter. In Liberia, during just one year of what would be twelve years of war, 1991 was as common as the year before it and the years after. There was fighting throughout the country, and more than two hundred thousand people, civilians mostly, had been killed. At least fifty died each day from starvation and disease. There were the unlucky ones, the people who were too poor to escape to neighboring countries or beyond, and then there were the foolish ones who had hung on too long, thinking that things would change or that the war would never touch them. Mary was one of the foolish.

As they drove out of the city, Mary could not ignore how the buildings on the main boulevard bore the violent marks of combat. When they passed the school where she used to teach, she allowed herself to look at the buildings' corpses, the shattered windows, the crumbling and blackened walls. Despite herself, she smiled as she thought about her former students, their eagerness and their laughter. She wondered what would become of them.

Monrovia once made sense, she thought to herself as the truck sped away from the downtown area. The avenues and streets had been modeled after those in the best cities in America. But on this early morning, there was no electricity. The truck's headlights and the glow of a few smoky oil-burning lamps that belonged to women trying to sell assorted wares along the side of the road were the only lights that cut through the gray haze.

Mary looked down at her children, half lying, half sitting on top of each other in the truck's cabin. Her eldest, her only daughter, Catherine, leaned her head against Mary's arm, but she was not asleep. Mary worried that Catherine might never have the opportunities she had. Catherine might never go to university, might never be a doctor . . . all the things she'd dreamed might be possible for her daughter.

Mary stopped herself from thinking about the long list of dreams. Instead, she slid down in her seat, trying to make Catherine more comfortable. Mary was tired. They were not yet out of Monrovia, and though Tapeta was not far—about a three-hour drive if the roads were good—she wanted to stay awake, in solidarity with James. She was nearly asleep when they approached a roadblock manned by soldiers from Doe's national army, the AFL. She watched two of the soldiers, around the age of twenty, approach the truck.

"How's the day?" James called out from the open window. Mary knew that it galled him to have to show these young men respect.

One soldier walked to the vehicle and stood in front of the headlights. He was a twig of a boy. His green uniform hung off his body and crumpled against the Kalashnikov that hung over his shoulder. When the soldier walked over to the passenger side, Mary grew nervous. The other soldier was at the driver's window. He looked in at the children and ran his eyes over the back of the truck.

"We are going to Gardnersville," James said. Gardnersville was just outside Monrovia, and the AFL still held the area, though just barely. The soldier said nothing. Mary knew what would come next. James pulled out a roll of bills and handed it to the soldier. The boy passed the money from one hand to the other, as if weighing it. Satisfied, he motioned to the skinny soldier to move the piece of wood that blocked the road.

"WHEN WE LEFT MONROVIA, it felt so easy. What seemed important before—our home, the objects—it was useless. Knowing how easy it was to just pick up and leave mocked all of the months that we had decided to stay in Monrovia. Do you understand?" Mary seemed to direct this question mostly to herself, but I nodded anyway. She looked at me, her eyes registering a vague sense of disappointment. "Every day, I think how very stupid we were, me and James. We did not realize that we were asking to be killed. We had the means to get out of Liberia altogether, but we lacked the courage and the will."

CHAPTER 7.
A Letter

THE SOUND OF PAULINE'S slippered feet scraping against the concrete floor pushed against the echoes of the clanging gates and muffled voices that played like a soundtrack in Rebibbia. It had been nearly two months since our first interview, and it seemed that this was the first time Pauline didn't want to talk. In truth, I wasn't paying attention to the lull in our conversation. I was too busy staring at her toes. They were short nubs that crossed over each other haphazardly. While it was typical for some people's toes to appear neglected, Pauline's managed to look downright abandoned, with thick yellow nails that curled back under themselves.

"You know," she said over the din of prison life, "after six years in this place, I am used to the sounds here. I think

I would go crazy without them. It's peaceful. And I am like a baby—all this activity soothes me to sleep." Her voice brought my eyes back to her face. Pauline was responding to a question that I had asked earlier, almost an hour ago. I was confused for a moment. Despite our many weeks working together, I was still getting accustomed to her style. Usually, she chatted away with ease about the small things: the weather, prison food, her workouts, and a yoga class that she was taking. Other times she was serious, instructive even. There were moments when stories burst from her—sometimes she would talk about her childhood or her business—but mostly she talked about books. She preferred philosophical tracts.

But today, Pauline was in a rare mood. I sat uncomfortably, witnessing her brooding quiet, waiting for yet another opportunity to wrap up our meeting.

"So," I started again, trying to sound casual, "I'm not sure when they will let me come back in, but let's try for next week. I'll write you and let you know when I'm coming."

Pauline winced. I had unintentionally hit a sore spot. She recovered quickly and gave me a cold look. "No. You stay for a while. I am not done yet."

I didn't want to sulk like a child, but I sat huffing and sighing in the chair as I waited for her to break her silence. Eventually, she showed me why she was preoccupied. She reached into the pocket of her sweatpants and pulled out a letter that bore the bruises of being handled too many times. She threw it toward the table that I was sitting at, but she missed the mark and the envelope landed on the floor with a loud *slap* that surprised me. I bent to pick it up but then wasn't sure if I should. I looked at Pauline. She had moved to the window. It was a reluctant invitation, so I picked up the letter, noticing the writer's small, sharp cursive; it looked young and masculine.

It was from her eldest son, Albert. It had arrived a few days earlier. Without salutation, the letter began, "I didn't think it was possible for you to disappoint me any more than you have. Once again you have proven me wrong. I am, as you have made me to be, your very stupid son. So, I write this very last letter to you to tell you that I am tired of being your son. You have ruined our lives and I hate you and will never forgive you for that. Don't write to me or call me and don't send your friends to come talk to me. You do not exist. You are not my mother as much as I am not your son. Do not reply. I insist."

Pauline told me that when it had first arrived, she had not been able to open it. So the letter with the tidy black script against the white envelope sat like a chorus of screaming accusations for a couple of days. She was in no hurry. And she kept putting off what she knew would be bad news. As she held off the truth for a little while, she thought of calling her son. She was thinking that she could say, honestly, that she had not read his letter, or she might lie and even say that she never received it. But she didn't. She knew that he would not answer his phone, accept her calls, or respond to any messages. No, he had already made his feelings clear during his previous visit to the prison.

I hadn't realized that Albert had come for a visit, but then again, Pauline would not have told me something like that, at least not after only two months of our knowing each other. Weeks later, she told me of the last time she had seen him, how he'd looked. "He was white." She smiled at what was clearly an inside joke. "He wore all white. White jeans, white shirt, white sneakers. You should have seen him," she marveled proudly.

Albert had just turned twenty. To Pauline, he was not quite a man, but Albert thought differently. He was tall and perhaps a bit too thin for her taste. He walked with the confident authority of someone who was at the beginning of his life and liked the road he had chosen for himself. Pauline thought of him as handsome, maybe too handsome, with his loose, soft curly hair, full lips, and wide-spaced eyes. She wasn't sure how her genes and those of her husband, Charles, had combined to create a kid as good-looking as Albert. He looked a bit like the very best of both of them, but mostly like himself.

But Pauline preferred not to think about her family, or what used to be her family. Allowing her mind to linger on them for too long made her agitated. I could see that she wrestled with her mind to come back to the present, to her body. Once, she had told me, "I don't mind being here. I am not like these other girls."

Other women, mostly from Africa, came and went. Some women remained at the prison for several months, and a few for a couple of years, but Pauline always stayed behind. She had gotten over her longing to get out of prison a while ago. "Better to be poor in prison than poor on the street," she would always tell people. She meant it, too. She didn't have any false impressions of what life after incarceration would look like, unlike most of the women around her. Pauline found their constant planning about the weeks, days, and years following their release from Rebibbia tedious. Nor did she set her dial to past events that she reflected on longingly. No, Pauline claimed that she would stay put in the present. But then Albert's letter arrived, challenging her to reconsider her convictions.

"Thinking about his letter . . . " she indicated with her chin to Albert's note, still in my hands. "How should I feel?" she asked, not really seeking an answer. Pauline wrinkled her face at me and shook her head slowly. "Don't give me your pity. Albert is an ungrateful child. He will change his mind in a matter of days." She snatched the letter out of my hands, jammed it into the envelope and then quickly stuck it in the waistband of her sweats.

I sat uncertain about what I should say or do, if anything. Moments like this—social interactions that require me to offer rational, firm, and balanced commiseration always leave me stymied. Usually, I overempathize. For a few minutes I listened to Pauline blame Charles and Albert for being too sensitive, for not being able to handle the difficulties that were a natural part of life. It was their weakness, their lack of vision, their inability to let her be who she was, that made her family suffer so. "The two of them make me tired." She said with some heaviness in her voice. I saw the truth of her words in her eyes.

Nevertheless, I had one more question. I wanted to ask why Albert was so angry with her. Clearly, she had recently done something to make him angry enough to sever ties, now after the years that he had kept in touch with her. Though I wanted to know, I was not going to ask yet. It was a mystery that I wasn't sure I would ever get a chance to solve. But I was certainly going to try.

"I'll see you next week." I called out but Pauline was already too far down the corridor to hear me.

CHAPTER 8.
Death, a Fragment

Mary could not remember what got her out of bed that night. Was it the shouting of Taylor's men or their gunshots? She had known they would be coming, but still, she had not prepared. Out of habit, she tied a piece of cloth around her chest, covering her T-shirt and leggings. In the dark, she ran across the yard to get the children from their room. She saw two silhouettes, their backs to the door.

"Get away from the window!" Her voice stumbled on its own anger, seeing her children exposed like that, so vulnerable to bullets. She jerked them up by their thin arms and traced her steps back across the courtyard of the compound. Something was not right. Confused, she stopped and looked around. It was night, but she could see women running from one room into the next, gathering children as they went. Suddenly, she remembered.

"Where's your sister?" she screamed at her two boys, Peter and Jacob, only five and three years old. Their eyes were mute with terror.

"Catherine!" Mary's yell came out of her throat as a high-pitched shriek.

"Catherine!" she shouted again. She listened to the sound of her voice knock against the tree in the courtyard and fall flat to the ground. She turned, frantic. Mary scanned the yard for a flash of her daughter's yellow sleepshirt.

Catherine would have gone with all the women who would barricade themselves behind Mama's, Mary's mother-in-law's, bedroom door, she thought. Mary moved toward the corner room. She gripped Peter and lifted Jacob to her hip; then, from the opposite direction, the blue paint of the side door caught her eye. Just then, Cousin Grace pushed past her, shoving Peter to the ground. Grace was heading toward Mama's door, but it was already closed and Mary knew that she and Grace would not make it in time.

"No, Grace, come this way!" Mary snatched Peter off the ground and turned to run, hoping that her cousin would follow. She ran out the side door, nearly tripping as she ran by the trough where the goats ate. Her thighs burned. Her right arm strained under Jacob's weight; she dragged Peter with her left. Finally, her feet came down hard on the rocky, uneven trail. The sharp smell of damp earth filled her nose, and she knew she was in the bush. She slowed her pace. It was quiet.

The trail led to a clearing that would put Mary out on the road. She knew this because it was the way to the market. If she took the path, she would not have any place to hide. She strained her eyes to look into the darkness off the trail, where the vegetation grew close together. The chest-high grass and bushes were so thick, they seemed to create their own dense heat.

Peter was breathing hard; Mary motioned for him to be quiet. Though he was five years old, he was big for his age. She had let go of his arm and placed her hand on his head. He was sweating and shivering, fear working over his body. She led him off the path.

The forest floor was softer than the trail. Little shrubs stuck out of the ground and pierced Mary's feet. From the direction of the house Mary heard male voices crying, "Maid service!" and, "We came to clean! Everyone outside!"

The voices dripped with sarcasm and liquor. She could not tell how many of them were in the house, but she imagined them swarming like ants, crawling through the house, breaking whatever stood in their way, crashing through doors and windows and maybe even walls. She raced for the nearest tree. She shoved her sons flat against its trunk and squatted, covering them with her body. Her chest burned, her breath a ragged, heavy panting.

"Please God, oh please God," she whispered over and over again. Her ears caught the sound of stew pots falling heavily to the concrete floor with a sharp metallic *clang*. Mary's stomach dropped when she heard the hysterical screams of women—that particular sound of fear that begins low and groggy, like a baby first waking from a nap, then grows into a hum before it shifts seamlessly into a vibrating buzz, causing the body to shake.

Catherine's face was just behind Mary's eyes as she closed them against the panicked cries of the women in the house. "Please spare my girl," she begged God. She squeezed her eyes tightly against the screams. Mary pictured Catherine hiding in a place only a clever eight-year-old girl would know about.

Mary's legs were shaking underneath her. She leaned against the boys with her full weight. Jacob had been sobbing quietly, but now his cry became louder. She turned him on her breast to quiet him. Her ears tried to dissect the sounds coming from the house. Was that Mama yelling? She thought she heard Isaac, Grace's seven-year-old son, screaming out for his mother. Some boys were laughing.

TWO WEEKS AFTER THEY arrived in Tapeta from Monrovia, the *rat-a-tat* of machine gunfire filtered through the leaves. Birds picked up the thud of mortar-rocket explosions in their wings and dropped it near the Johnson home. Mary and James began to count how many days it would take for the rebels to reach them. When James's entire family decided it would take fewer than three days, the Johnson men told their mother, wives, sisters, and aunties goodbye with little emotion, piled into the truck, and went into the forest.

Thinking that Taylor's rebels would come from the west, the men hid in the jungle and slept under the trees, hoping to protect their families, preparing to fight Taylor's men away from the children. In the meantime, the plan was for the women to gather their things and head east, toward the border of the Ivory Coast.

The men had miscalculated. The NPFL, Taylor's men, were already upon them. They appeared silently at first, leaving only empty beer bottles, cigarette butts, and footprints.

And now it was too late.

A LOUD MECHANICAL SCREECH broke through the chaos. The sound hit Mary in the stomach. Ripping Jacob away from her, she staggered away from the tree.

She felt Peter grab onto her leg and she tripped over a bush. Bile came up through her mouth and nose. It felt as if fire ants had bitten the back of her throat. Lying flat on her stomach in the mud, she sobbed. She did not want to look up. She already knew that a white Toyota had pulled up to the house. Inexperienced feet popped the clutch too soon and lingered too long on the gas pedal. The stick shift was temperamental, but it was the screech from the worn-out brake pads that broke the news: The men had found James. They were driving his truck.

Even from where Mary and the boys were sitting, they could hear how roughly their father and uncles were pulled from the truck: Days later, when Mary returned to the house, she would see that bones had been broken quickly, T-shirts bloodied, pants and shorts soiled. But from her hiding place that morning, she was haunted mostly by the sounds from the women of the house. They were wailing, their shrieks flung upward like tiny needles piercing the sky. But the god that they called out to did nothing. Later, surviving neighbors, strangers to Mary, told her in flat tones that Taylor's men had spat in the faces of old women and taunted girls who could have been their sisters. The rebels broke noses with closed fists before finally lining them up, all fifteen of them: men, women, girls, boys, babies.

In the forest, Mary enfolded her boys' heads into her body as she tried to shield their ears from the sounds of the metal butts of guns hitting flesh. Beneath her, the ground vibrated with dragging skin, kicking feet, heads being pushed into the earth, and teeth falling out against rocks. The cries were indistinguishable—she could not tell if it was men or women, cousins, or her husband. Mud was stuffed in the victims' mouths as all of them begged for their lives, to no avail. One by one, they were executed.

The sickening scent of warm blood mingling with dirt, human feces, and gunfire wafted through the air. It would stay in Mary's nose for months. But despite what she could smell and see, it was the pleading screams, so sharp with terrorized hysteria, that would haunt her most. Days and weeks later, as she and the boys slowly made their way to the road out of Tapeta, toward the border of the Ivory Coast, and even later, many years on, Mary wore those screams like scars. They were permanent.

CHAPTER 9.
Family Sublime

AS WAS HER HABIT, Pauline scratched intently at her scalp, just under her braids, as if feeling for the spot that would bring her past forward accurately. She was thinking about Albert's childhood, his move from Uganda, and his growing up in Italy.

She seemed disoriented. She couldn't recall Albert at that age; she had only brief, blurry glimpses of him at different stages of his life: as a tightly clenched newborn, all crumpled and tense from his entry into the world, as a chatty and curious boy of three or four with an impossibly large head, and as a quiet adolescent who preferred the company of his father or his aunty or his Italian schoolmates over that of his mother.

These snapshots didn't reveal much to Pauline about her son or how he'd grown up. The truth was, she was a distracted mother. She wasn't like some of the women around her at Rebibbia, who talked about their children as if they were tracking a sporting event. Pauline couldn't recite Albert's first word or remember when he'd taken his first step or when his first tooth had fallen out. She'd never asked about the marks he earned in school or his favorite subjects. She didn't even know what kind of music, books, and food he liked and disliked.

"Albert was always independent from me, and that was good for both of us," Pauline told me. Besides, Pauline said plainly, "Albert always preferred Joyce."

Pauline had told me enough about her family for me to know that she must have been angry that Albert chose Joyce over her. Whenever Pauline spoke of her tall and rather unsightly older sister, with her thick glasses and shy manner, she seemed to spit out her name in disgust. Pauline believed Joyce had never known how to live in the world and had always huddled under her bible, trying to save the souls of dirty street children.

Before Albert was born in Uganda, Pauline brought Joyce up to Kampala from the nearby town of Entebbe. Having Joyce live with her gave her sister a broader purpose in life—Pauline was confident of that. After all, she wondered, how could Joyce ever have loved those nameless urchins—those mission projects—as much as she came to love Albert? Pauline thought that she had rescued her sister from the disappointments of charity work. "Strangers could never be as important as family. She had to leave Entebbe."

Whenever Joyce would ask to return to work with her church, Pauline wouldn't trouble over her sister's tears; instead, she would demonstrate how pointless Joyce's church work was. Now, she imagined their conversations and acted them out for me: She remembered how Joyce would sit quietly on the sofa as Pauline paced the floor, and she used a whiny voice to mimic Joyce's requests to leave Kampala. Why, Pauline wondered out loud to me, would Joyce rather care for people who were just going to use her time and throw her away after they got what they wanted: a bit of food, a free bible that they couldn't read, the useless skill of writing their own names when they couldn't afford the paper to write them on?

According to Pauline, she was a realist—she didn't trust what she couldn't get with her own two hands. In that way, she was loyal to her own experience. She learned early that the combined forces of strength and will were what created change. "This and this," she would say, holding out first her left and then her right fist.

Joyce, on the other hand, believed in ghosts, saints, and miracles. For Pauline, beseeching, praying, and singing to some faceless entity was a lazy person's way to avoid the hard work of confronting life's challenges. "What is religion but weakness?" she once asked me. "Religion makes people stupid and complacent about their pathetic lives. I am not the only intelligent person to think that. You know, scholars say that all the time," she told me with great conceit. It disgusted Pauline, the idea of faith—the idea of waiting for something, people's preaching about a man that to Pauline was nothing but a mere phantom.

Pauline's hatred of what she perceived as weakness must have been the reason she reacted so strongly when she realized that her sister, taking care of Albert daily, had started reading to him from the Bible and taking him to church in Kampala while Pauline was working. They had been living at her in-laws' house, and when she discovered what Joyce had been doing, she dragged her sister into the courtyard of the family home and, as Pauline's husband, Charles, and his mother looked on from a bench on the veranda, beat Joyce until she was breathless and exhausted. As her sister lay prone, her face as deep into the cement ground as Pauline could bury it, Pauline went calmly into Joyce's small room and took her bible off the nightstand. Kicking over a pot of food that was cooking on the outside stove, Pauline recalled triumphantly, she "burned that damned book."

Pauline recounted to me how she watched with pleasure as the pages, all annotated with her sister's delicate script, curled and floated away in dark, charred wisps. Then she turned to look at Albert. "He was blubbering. I had never seen him like that; his whole face was wet—mucus and tears." Pauline noticed the strain that her mother-in-law had to use to hold him back from hitting his mother; she smiled at the memory. "He might have been three or four or maybe even two years old." Whatever his age, Pauline knew that Albert was going to be a strong boy.

What Pauline never understood about that day, though, was why her sister didn't fight back. "She was so big that it was like a child trying to butcher a cow with a kitchen knife,"

Pauline would later say about the fight. From that moment on, Joyce never spoke to Pauline directly, never showed any emotion when they were in the same room, never looked at her. The only time Pauline saw her sister cry was when Joyce said goodbye to Albert six years later, when they moved to Rome.

But, after nearly two years in Rome, Charles managed to persuade Joyce—who was worried about living under the same roof as her violent sister—to come live with them, as well as convince the Italian government to let her stay for the length of his residency at the university La Sapeniza, where he was studying to be a mathematician. But as Charles's studies wore on and on, Joyce went quietly back to Uganda.

Pauline remembered that while she was indifferent to her sister's departure, both Charles and Albert seemed to take it very hard. Pauline hated how for weeks after Joyce left, they treated her as if she were a stranger in their house. "Charles should have married Joyce; he would have been much happier with a quiet girl." Pauline told me more than once.

If she thought of her former husband now, she did so with a combination of pity and an anger that leaned closer toward annoyance than toward bitterness. She didn't regret their lives in Rome before their arrest, and she certainly didn't think that it was her fault that Charles was in prison. "My son can blame me all he wants for his father's arrest. Why not?" She shrugged her shoulders. "Albert has done that so often in the past."

Even when Charles didn't work for Pauline, he had known about and benefited from her business, so she didn't feel bad. "We ate rice or potatoes for every meal, and suddenly we were eating meat? Charles never asked—he just ate." Pauline often laughed at the poverty of her early days in Rome; in fact, she seemed amused by her entire situation, including, if not especially, her and her husband's imprisonment. Before his transfer, Charles had been held in Rebibbia's male prison, just next door. According to Pauline, in many ways they were closer now, had more in common, than they had during the two entire decades of marriage preceding their incarceration. In the early days she had imagined him pacing his cell, reading his books, and writing letters to his family, just as she was doing. But she rarely thought of him now.

"I have not heard from Charles for a long time." His very last letter had arrived two years ago. She still had it, but she didn't need to read it to recall the words: "He couldn't be married to me anymore. He said it was too difficult."

Charles had finally come to the conclusion that Pauline had known was inevitable from the moment she met him. From the very beginning, she had wondered if she loved Charles, or if she could ever grow to love him. They had certainly lasted longer than she had thought they would. But with a few simple lines, he ended their marriage—or at least told her that he did not consider himself married to her anymore. His sister in Kampala was making certain that their divorce was legal and final. Really, it was for the best. There was no way for them to go on—it was not even worth pretending anymore. They had stayed together not for the sake of the children, but maybe, Pauline thought, out of laziness and because of the fact that she had come to know Italy as her home, and her immigration status was tied to Charles's studies and her position as his wife.

This was Pauline's second time in an Italian prison. The first time had been many years before, during an investigation for racketeering. Pauline had been held, along with Albanian and Italian men whom she worked with. She had known the evidence in the case was weak, and, though she had been running drugs at the time, she had not been involved directly in any protection racket. Still, Albert had been young and taken away from her. Charles had still been naive and hadn't known what she was doing. He had fought hard to have Albert returned to him, but there was nothing he could do for Pauline. She had to save herself, as she felt she always did. "I played it stupid. And after a few months, I was allowed to go back home to our small apartment near the university. Simple."

But this time, it was not going to be so simple. She was going to be in prison for ten years, and Charles was too, but she was now without either a husband or a son. And her daughter, Isabel, had written off Pauline years ago. This time, unlike the last time she had been in Rebibbia, she would be sent back to Uganda after she completed her sentence. So when she went back to Kampala, she would go alone.

TURNING AWAY FROM HER thoughts, Pauline focused on a shift in the background noise. A multitude of women's voices and laughter rose and flooded the corridor, marking a shift in the prison's routine. "It's lunchtime," she said, visibly cheered by the prospect of food. "After lunch I'll have a nap, and then I'll go train. You know, I have a race coming up soon." I nodded. Pauline stood up and gave her legs a shake at the thought of running. I took it as a signal. She was done talking for the day.

CHAPTER 10.
Tempting Matrons

I FELT A PRESSING need to find Albert. If I could meet him, I could get a better sense of Pauline, perhaps understand what guided her through life. I wanted to know more. In a way, I *had* to know, because in the months we had spent speaking with each other, Pauline had kept me at a safe distance, at least until this morning when she showed me Albert's letter. Yet I knew that today would not change our relationship. I was certain that come tomorrow, next week, or even two months from now, she would still tell me the same four stories of her glory days as a drug dealer. As if she were creating a ten-minute trailer for a Roger Corman film, she could magnificently re-count her ascent from selling a kilo of marijuana out of her apartment for a few hundred dollars to masterfully brokering drug shipments that yielded thousands of dollars.

But more than wanting to get to know her—and I did—I also wanted to get behind the stories that she told me, but I simultaneously was too scared and felt too guilty to dig so deeply into her life. And I no longer wanted to speak with her on her terms only. Albert could provide me with a different perspective—that of having the infamous Ugandan for a mother.

I got up. I decided to start my search for Albert right there in the prison. I had an idea of who might be able to help me. Maria was an *educatora,* and since my first day at Rebibbia, she had been my official contact. She treated me in that way in which people who work in undesirable and mysterious institutions (prisons, mental hospitals) greet visitors from the outside. That is to say, she didn't like me, or at least she didn't seem to like my being around. To Maria, I was a burden that the director of the prison and the minister of justice had dumped on her.

For me, Maria was an obstacle. She mediated whom I could speak to, when, and for how long. I didn't *not* like her, but part of her job was to make doing mine difficult. However, I did admire her. Maria was tough and unpretentious. She had a sense of fair play. She could not be charmed or cajoled in any way. If I wanted something from her, I would have to be straightforward and firm. Her assistance would not come without a high price, though; I would have to leave my dignity as down payment.

I found Maria standing in a plume of smoke outside the administrative office. She smoked deliberately and without sophistication, holding her cigarette between her thumb and index finger.

"Good afternoon." I said, as I got a bit closer to her. She was standing on one leg, leaning against the building, with the other leg bent, her foot resting on the wall. She was wearing dangerously high heels. I waited for her to acknowledge me.

"*Buona sera,*" she replied. A thick stream of smoke came from someplace deep within Maria's lungs. She took a long drag on the cigarette before crossing one arm over her rounded stomach and flicking it in my direction. There was the suggestion of disgust. I watched the cigarette fly like a wad of spit in the air.

Maria stood straight up then, smoothed her skirt, and fluffed her hair. I could see that she had dyed it recently. The color was a reddish burgundy, a few shades darker and more vibrant than the brown color she'd had a few weeks before. She may have been in her fifties, but it was hard to tell. She was a matronly temptress, like a shorter, rounder Sophia Loren at forty. I never saw her in pants; she seemed to always wear a skirt, a tight sweater, heels, and a few pieces of gold jewelry. Her fingernails always matched the color of her lipstick; I thought that was an especially nice touch.

"Are you done for the day?" When Maria spoke, her voice churned gravel. It was at once cruel and seductive.

"I am. But I was hoping you could tell me about Pauline's son." I watched her face to see how she would handle my request.

"Why?" Maria didn't look through me so much as she looked past me. "Does Pauline know that you are asking about him?" She didn't wait for an answer and headed toward her office.

I followed and walked confidently next to her. In the oversize concrete hallway, the *clip* of our heels made an inharmonious racket, which in turn made Maria walk even more quickly, moving a few paces ahead of me. She was a short woman with strong, solid calves. My legs were longer, but I couldn't keep up. I watched her go into the office that she shared with two other social workers.

When I entered the room, she was standing by a desk, thumbing through some papers. She was facing the door, waiting for me. "He is a student. La Sapienza, the Faculty of Pharmacy." She stopped there satisfied that she had given me the information that I was looking for.

"Albert is in the faculty of engineering," I corrected her.

"Oh, yes, engineering." Maria moved to her chair and sat down. "Does Pauline know that you are asking about him? Because I am sure she could tell you what you want to know."

To an outsider, this was a casual exchange between two women. But upon further inspection, someone might have noticed Maria's smirk and my annoyance. She was digging her heels into the ground. I knew I would be the first person to cave. I had no choice. Even if she knew nothing, I had still set the wheels in motion. Maria was not going to let me live this down so easily.

"No, Pauline doesn't know that I am asking," I leveled, "and I'm not sure if I'm going to tell her."

"Fine." Maria waved me off. "I really don't want to get into this mess. Don't tell me any more. A few years ago, he worked someplace near Piazza dell'Orologio. That's it. That is all I know."

I tried to not be suspicious. Maria knew a lot about the inmates; it was her job and she seemed to be as close as anyone could be to Pauline. "Really?" I asked.

She rolled her eyes. "Really. Now go." She had already turned her back to me. I started toward the door silently, lost in the thought of the futility of staking out a huge plaza.

"Hey, American," Maria called out, using the dreaded nickname she had given me when I first arrived, "be careful. You don't want to get too close. These women have their reasons for being here—don't forget."

I knew her warning was coming a little too late. "Okay" was the only response I could manage.

CHAPTER 11.
Note to Self

AS IT TURNED OUT, I was going to have to put my search for Albert on hold. When I arrived home that day, I realized that I had an even bigger problem brewing. My flatmate, Connie, came rushing to the door the moment I entered it.

"Asale! You have to come into my room. I want you to meet someone." Connie's checks were flushed bright red, and her eyes seemed out of focus. She spun quickly into the darkened front room, leaving the two French doors open behind her. I followed tentatively.

As I stepped into the room, my foot immediately made contact with a heavy glass bottle. I couldn't see it, but I heard it skitter across the floor. Connie's laughter ricocheted off the high ceilings, high-pitched, hysterical, and intoxicated.

"Connie, it's three in the afternoon. You could open the curtains, let some light in here." My flatmate was an alcoholic.

She'd rejected so many offers of help that I was past the point where her drunkenness mattered anymore. I hardly saw her. She woke late each morning and was generally passed out by midnight. There were times, however, when she would emerge from the bottle and present herself, clean and sober. It was as if she drank herself to such a low point that even she was disgusted with herself, so when she hit bottom she came back up fighting. She would thoroughly clean the apartment, pick up where she'd left off with her business of importing computer parts from China to Italy, and try to renew her custody battle against her ex-husband.

I usually stayed out of Connie's way, and I almost never entered her room. I didn't know where to put my eyes when I did. I'd focus on the windows that led out to the terrace. The brilliant sunlight tried to sneak around the edges of the heavy fabric that she'd drawn across them. Old computers littered every surface, papers were stacked high on a massive desk that took up most of the room. Cheap old calendars decorated the walls. I wanted to throw the curtains back, clean up, and release Connie from her time warp. But the apartment belonged to her. Connie used the expansive living room as her quarters, and I rented the small back bedroom near the bathroom. When we did meet, it was in the communal spaces of the foyer, the galley kitchen, or the hallway. I despised living here. But it was affordable and near my favorite place in Rome, the park Villa Ada.

"Come, Asale, sit next to Roberto," Connie shouted in Italian, pounding the sofa with her hand. A gangly, dark-haired man in his late twenties or early thirties was there, holding a glass with two hands. He was staring at a dark space across the room. I hadn't noticed before, but there was another man, about the same age as Roberto, sitting on the floor. He didn't appear to be drinking. He held up his hand in a half salute and announced, "Daniele." I doubted that he could see me nod my head at his introduction.

"What is going on?" I asked Connie in English. We were foreign women, Connie and I. To our elderly, provincial neighbors who patrolled our building, it didn't matter that I was from the United States or that Connie was from England. Since she was Chinese and I was some unspecified brown person, we lived under an added layer of scrutiny. Having two strange men in our flat would be grist for the mill.

Though I thought some of my neighbors' suspicions were flat-out racist, I knew that under the circumstances, Connie and I seemed a bit odd: We were two single women who lived in our own flat in a country where unmarried people mostly still lived with their parents. Likewise, neither one of us had a clear day job. I may have "gone to work" every day—doing my research, going to Rebibbia or another prison, visiting and interviewing officials or spending time at the library at the United Nations Interregional Crime and Justice Research Institute—but I set my own hours. And then there was the fact that Connie was drunk most of the time.

Connie gave me a big toothy grin. Her face was alight with an enthusiasm that would have been infectious in just about anyone besides her. She was a compact, homely woman with square, mannish features and flat, wide teeth and skin that resembled curdled milk. But despite her looks and her drinking, she had a charming innocence about her that was impossible not to like.

"I am helping you with your research! They are here to talk to you. They are *Carabinieri*." She was pleased with herself and, I could tell, getting ready to launch into the story of how she'd met them. But I did not want to know how she'd become acquainted with these two police sitting in the room.

"Listen, I'm not interested in speaking with them. I'm busy right now." I started to walk out. And then I thought of Pauline. Was she still keeping tabs on me? Would she ever find out that I'd had the police in my flat? I gave Connie a long cold look. It occurred to me then that I had never told her, or even the few friends I had in Italy, about how I spent my days in Rome. Did she listen in on my phone calls? Did she read my letters or journals after I left the house each day? It wasn't a secret that I went to the prison to interview people, but the kind of people—who they were and where they were from—was what I wanted to protect. With my suspicions running high, I asked Connie, "What did you tell them I am was doing, exactly?"

"I told them that you wanted to know how they caught criminals!" She was so matter-of-fact, so eager with her response. I could not entertain her offer. It was too risky; even if Pauline or any of the other inmates never found out, I knew that I could be endangering any trust that people had in me not to speak to the police, and in such an intimate setting as my home. Before I could say no, Connie returned to her loud, heavily accented Italian and told Roberto, "She can't join us right now. But maybe later?" Her eyes darted up to mine for confirmation.

I nodded my head and quickly left Connie's room. I wasn't halfway down the dark hallway before I saw an envelope with a U.S. stamp on it. Recognizing the hard writing, I picked up the letter and judged the contents by its weight: thin, flat, and likely to reveal no significant emotions or revelations. It would not be the first time a letter from my mother would disappoint me. I hardly spoke to her, but still I longed for us to be part of each other's lives.

I stuffed the envelope into my pocket. I headed for my bedroom. I turned the door handle slowly, preparing myself for what was inside. The room was pink. Not a pleasant sunset or coral pink, but a hot pink, a pink of plastic toys and sugary candy. It was a color that stirred anxiety. In the room were two miniature twin beds pushed together, an imposing armoire that filled the space like a giant block of glossed wood, a small glass-topped side table that I used as my desk, and a metal folding chair. With a window that provided little light, the austere room was perfect for an adolescent nun. The open door channeled the sounds of conversation and raucous laughter from Connie's room. Without putting down my bag, I fled to Villa Ada.

CHAPTER 12.
Speaking in Tongues

EACH TIME MARY, JACOB, and Peter made it to the relative safety of the Ivorian border, something always pushed or drew them back into Liberia. The first time, it was the men guarding the border who turned Mary and her boys away. When it was clear that she hadn't brought much money and had nothing of value to barter in the little bundle of clothes that she carried, they sent her in the direction from which she had come.

Not long after returning to Liberia, Mary met a woman who, like her, had been trying to cross the border. About the same age as Mary, the woman was also a mother. She carried an infant so young and so small that Mary at first did not notice the child pressed against his mother's chest. But traveling with the baby was not what was remarkable about this woman. It was that, in contrast with so many people around her, this woman talked, and talked, and talked. She seemed to comment on everything: the shade of blue in the sky, the shape of her child's ear, the sight of a bird carrying a pinch of food in its mouth.

Mary, like the others who sought shelter in the dilapidated school on the edge of a nameless village, sat impassively as the woman tossed her disjointed thoughts out into the endlessly flowing stream of words, as if she were hoping to catch just enough of them to assemble a meaningful truth. Mary worried that the woman might be insane, so she wanted to keep her distance.

This crazy woman had arrived on Mary's third evening at the school. She came with a few women, some small children, and two old men. They were weary but brought news and obliged the villagers and the displaced with the stories of what they had seen along the way: abandoned homes, burned-down farms, dead bodies decomposing in the bush. Mary listened, but she already knew the outcome of the travelers' tales. As did all stories carried on the backs of those who escaped villages, this one would end with the narrators' telling the gathered crowd to leave soon, because on their heels followed the uncertainty of the men with guns. From one day to the next, their lives could change with the arrival of soldiers. If they were lucky, the rebels would only be hungry and would just eat all of their food or maybe pilfer a few of their possessions: a plastic bowl and spoon, a bible, a pair of shoes? Or would these men kill a couple villagers to make a point? Would they rape the women and girls, take a few as "brides," and maybe a handful of children, too, as unwilling conscripts?

Mary watched the speakers carefully, trying to determine, without asking how long and how far they had come, whether, like most of the people standing before them, they had completed the cycle of fleeing and returning to their home until the rebels or the army had tired of the place and burned it down to the ground—or, worse, occupied it, sullying the land and the memories attached to it. Mary took in their shabby and dirty clothes, the meaningless bundles that they transported on their heads or in their hands, the broken flip-flops, the dusty bare feet. She scanned each of their faces and knew at once what she was looking at.

"There was something in their eyes, something unusual, like stones that float in a river. It was as if what their eyes had seen didn't make sense to them. *I know, I know,* I kept saying to myself." Even though she had not seen her reflection in nearly a year, Mary knew that she looked exactly the same way.

She waited until the crowd started slowly dispersing before she slipped away quietly to get water. She had already been thinking that she would leave the shelter of the small school to head back toward the border. If that didn't work, she was considering trying to get to Monrovia.

She had gone back to the compound in Tapeta after she had fled that first night, but she had found the house standing like an empty shell. Neighbors had been kind enough to remove the bodies, burying them or burning them back near the garden, which had been trampled and destroyed. But the neighbors had also, along with the soldiers, looted the place. When they saw her, a few people had stepped forward to return found photographs, a small cooking pot, a schoolbook that had belonged to somebody else's child. Mary had accepted all of these things but hadn't said a word about Peter's T-shirt that a little girl was wearing, nor had she gotten cross when she saw an old man wearing her sandals. After all, these people had lost everything, too.

At first, Mary had gone back to Tapeta to look for Catherine. Most of the people who had tended to the dead couldn't tell her if they had seen Catherine's body, but one man said he was certain that she had not been among them. When he described Catherine to prove that he knew which girl Mary was speaking of, it was enough for Mary to believe that she was still alive, even though the man had not seen Catherine following the night of the attack.

After a day or two at the house, Mary decided to head farther north, to the border. It was closer than going back to Monrovia, which was nearly four hours away, and the roads leading there were growing increasingly dangerous. Mary hoped that Catherine would be traveling with adults who would be smart enough to head in the opposite direction from the capital. Mary herself had followed her instinct all the way to the border and then back to this little village halfway between Tapeta and the Ivorian border, hoping that somewhere along the way she would find Catherine.

So when she heard a new arrival, this crazy woman, talking to the visitors about a home that took in lost and orphaned children, Mary rushed to her side and listened intently as the woman recalled her journey to the place, the family who ran it, and the help from the foreigners that seemed to keep the place going. The crazy woman had come from there two days before; she'd been looking for her own lost children: three daughters and a son. When she hadn't found them there, she'd been told that she might try a refugee camp in the Ivory Coast, so that was where she was heading next.

The woman and the visitors spoke in Lower Gio. Mary could follow just enough of their dialect to understand most of what they were saying. But when she tried to ask the woman if she had seen a girl who matched Catherine's description, Mary's tongue felt like a steel plate in her mouth.

CHAPTER 13.
The Branches and the Vine

OF MY EARLIEST MEMORIES, the day the police came to arrest my mother is the sharpest in my mind. Frankly, it came as no surprise. We had all been quietly expecting it for months.

We lived upstairs in the last of a row of apartments. Whenever anyone climbed the stairs and made their way down the hall, we could feel the vibrations of their feet pounding on the cheap cement that held our building together. So even before the police reached our door, my mother had scooped up my younger brother, turned off the television, and guided my identical twin sister, Lira, and me into the back of the apartment. We had practiced this drill many times in the past few days. Anytime my mother heard someone on the stairs, she ushered us quickly into her bedroom and told us to hide under the bed. While we were under there, my mother would rock my one-year-old brother back and forth in front of a poster of a peacock that was above his crib. I would stare, as if hypnotized, at the back of my mother's feet as they moved lightly to the left and to the right. Eventually she would break my trance with a relieved "Okay, you can get out from under there."

But not this time.

I was asleep when my mother opened the door to the waiting policemen, so I will never know for certain how they finally caught her. I guess they possessed something my mother never had—patience. They didn't bang down the door. They didn't coax my mother out with sweet negotiations. After they knocked and called out her name, they waited a little while and then headed back toward the stairs. That's where they stopped to have a smoke or two.

My mother must have taken her usual precautions when she went to the living room to look out the window, but I am not sure what made her actually open the front door to peek her head out. The policemen spotted her, and my mother, never one for theatrics, didn't put up a fight. When they took her to the station, she was barefoot and still carrying my brother on her hip. She was crying, which may explain why she forgot to mention to anyone that her twin daughters were still under her bed, alone in an empty apartment. When my grandmother arrived, well past midnight, she found us there asleep, hands clasped, our faces buried in the thick green shag carpet. We were five years old.

MY MOTHER, REBECCA, DIDN'T know how to be a fugitive. She lived in plain sight. She was raised as a shy middle-class girl who in the late 1960s found her purpose in life as an antiwar intellectual, a Gothic poet, an artist. When she met my father in high school, she had honed the talent of applying thick black eye makeup and wearing black dresses and long black velvet capes. In my father she saw an apparition. She convinced herself that he, too, had the soul of a poet, when in fact all evidence pointed to his being a young man who was lost in a world of wandering ambition and the desire for easy money.

They ran away to Mexico to get married shortly after my mother became pregnant with my sister and me. By the time she was in the hospital, pushing two babies out of her womb, my father was in federal prison for smuggling heroin into the United States. It didn't take long for their relationship to unravel.

I am not sure if my father had already been selling drugs when he first met my mother, but it is likely. When I was young, I had a very vague sense of the kind of household I had been born into. But for all that I didn't know about my father, I took solace in the facts that I had about my mother. While Dad was in the business of smuggling and selling drugs, my mother, who never so much as smoked or drank alcohol, was only caught in its crosshairs. It would take years before she developed a criminal habit all her own.

At the time of her arrest, Rebecca was a single mother of three with a low-wage job as a hospital aide. She couldn't make her checks spread out over the month, so she turned to public assistance. She faced a difficult choice: quit her job and accept meager welfare benefits, or keep working and maintain her dignity but come up short month after month? And then there was her boyfriend Pete, my brother's dad, who yo-yoed in and out of her life whenever she got paid.

When she decided that she would collect welfare *and* keep her job, she may or may not have realized that she was committing fraud. It wasn't until she became aware that the public assistance, combined with her wages, would still not cover rent, food, and Pete's bets at the track that I remember her writing what she called "bad checks."

In all manner of stores that sold food and accepted checks—which is to say, all of them back then—my mother would wait calmly as the clerk looked through a long list of names of people who had previously passed bad checks at the establishment. I remember the lists being typed up on sheets of white paper (computers were not used then). Some lists were so thick and the print was so small that the clerk had to thumb through them like the pages of a book. And the wait would be interminable.

Whenever my mother was told to leave the store, Lira and I handled the disappointment of having to leave our candy behind like any five-year-olds would have. We would whimper our protests as our mother steered us out by our arms, one twin on each side. When she was frustrated, and she often was, she would dig her nails deeper into our flesh, leaving bloody half-moon indents. Soon, we knew to avoid the candy aisle altogether.

This went on for months. Each time an overworked clerk rejected us, our family traveled farther away from home to do our shopping. I was too young to know that it was embarrassing to have to leave a basket of food at the register. We were hungry. If my sister and I could have eaten our shame, I would have eaten mine raw and with both hands.

CHAPTER 14.
Finding Albert

It was March when I found Albert. He was standing outside the optometrist shop where he worked. He was on a mobile phone, the quiet participant in the conversation. His eyes closed, his face was pointing up toward the sun. He looked serene. I could only guess that he resembled his father, because there was nothing about his features that brought Pauline to mind. When he spoke, though, he was all her. Like his mother, he paced the sidewalk, gesturing excitedly with his hands. I couldn't hear what he was saying, but the conversation was punctuated with short bursts of laughter. Even from where I was standing, almost directly across the street from him, it was obvious that he was casual, confident, and amiable. He didn't seem to be the type of guy who had a mother and a father sitting in prison.

I watched, not sure what I was supposed to do. I was fairly certain that he was the guy I was looking for, but I am really good at doubting even the surest things, so my mind filled with questions. Finally, I reasoned, the odds were low that there would be two black men of college age working in Piazza Dell'Orologio.

Albert got off the phone, and I prepared myself to cross to street to make my introductions. But a deliveryman from what must have been a nearby café got to Albert first and handed him a white plastic bag. They exchanged a brief, friendly pat on the back before Albert went inside the shop.

I groaned internally. I'm no good at stakeouts—I'm too impatient. So if I wanted to meet him, I would have to go inside the shop. I dreaded the mere thought of it. Maybe, I tried to convince myself, I could come back near closing time and pretend to bump into him. But then, I didn't know what time the shop closed, nor what time Albert would leave. What I did know was that if I walked away, went home, went window shopping, or sat in the park, I would come up with a million excuses for why I didn't need to meet Albert that day, or perhaps any day.

When it comes to making introductions, I am weighed down by insecurities, which is ironic given that I chose to be a cultural anthropologist—someone who devotes all her time to being among people, learning from them, and asking them questions; and who sometimes willingly and shamelessly makes linguistic mistakes or cultural faux pas, or breaches social etiquette in the pursuit of humanistic knowledge and multicultural understanding.

But finally my curiosity outweighed my timidity. I crossed the street and went inside the shop. There was nothing, not a bell or a buzzer or anything else, to mark my arrival. I was surprised that the room was dark and empty of any furniture except a few display cases pushed up against the walls. Only a handful of eyeglasses were on exhibit, so I busied myself with looking at them. I caught sight of a white coat flapping in my direction the minute I leaned in to touch a pair of frames.

"Good afternoon. May I help you?" He spoke in Italian. Without looking up, I already knew that it was not Albert; the voice had the richness of an older man's. I froze. Suddenly, it was clear that this was a very bad idea. I could not just come out and ask to speak to Albert, because then I would have to explain how I knew about him. Which might mean that he would be in a position to tell his boss how his mother, a mother he probably never spoke of, knew me.

I smiled politely at the Italian man who was now in front of me. "Are you looking for some glasses?" he asked in English this time.

I was embarrassed, but he couldn't know why. I wanted out, but leaving now would only make a scene. So I let him show me some glasses, but I kept one eye on the dark green curtain that separated the staff-only part of the store from the customers. Absentmindedly, I put on a pair.

"Oh, now those look nice," the optometrist said confidently. His voice brought my eyes to my face in the mirror in front of me. I saw that I was wearing a pair of glasses that were black, but the insides were red. The two-toned effect was dramatic and a bit startling. I looked nothing like I felt. I actually looked mature. I temporarily forgot the real reason why I was in the store and found myself contemplating the frames.

"They're nice, but I don't know." I was more than hesitant. The glasses were made by an Italian high-fashion design firm that I was certain was beyond my budget. I had not come in to spend money, but I was just the type of person who would, if pressed too hard by a salesperson.

"No, really, these suit you. Just one moment, please." The man went over to the curtain and spoke softly. My heart was thudding loudly in my ears. I turned away from the curtain and focused on the mirror in front of me. I waited for Albert to come out, but instead a young woman closer to my age, in her mid- to late twenties, walked into the room. She considered my face from a distance and said to me, "The glasses are good, but let's soften them." She reached into a drawer and pulled out a similar pair, but lighter in color. I put them on and she smiled.

I snapped out of my retail trance, and my mind went back to my task. I didn't care about the glasses or the money anymore. I was too anxious. In a way, because I had thought I was so close to meeting Albert, I was disappointed that I hadn't. Of course, another part of me knew that I had been granted a break. "Let me think about it. I'll come back." The woman gave me a look of disapproval. I knew that in Italy this was hardly done. People were more decisive when it came to purchasing things—especially after they had tried something on and taken up as much time as I had in a shop. As far as the clerk was concerned, the glasses were mine. I had put my fingerprints all over them.

I stepped out of the store, keenly aware that I was at a disadvantage. By leaving, I had made it impossible to go back, and now I'd have to devise a new plan for meeting Albert. I had told myself that meeting him would lead me to have a fuller picture of his mother, but really, if I was going to be honest with myself, I wanted to see if we were the same in any way. Albert was a little younger than I was, but still, I had to admit that I wanted to befriend him. For the first time, I had been given the opportunity to meet someone who might share the same sorts of secrets and shame that I had.

I turned around and walked back to the shop. I would look crazy, but it was either this or sitting outside, waiting to pounce on Albert the moment he left the building. This time, I was determined to not play games. I was going to go in there and ask for him—to hell with my fears.

THE YOUNG WOMAN WAS standing near the display case where I had been just ten minutes before. When she saw me, she smiled triumphantly; then the curtain drew back. The man in the white coat appeared again. But this time, when he pushed his way through the fabric, I saw him—Albert. He was sitting cross-legged, holding a pair of glasses in his hands, adjusting the fit. His eyes caught mine just as the curtain fell back into place. Though I was now staring at the dark-green divider, I could still see Albert sitting there. I felt the optometrist's and the salesclerk's eyes on me; I faltered. "Okay, yes, I will get the glasses," I said.

The woman sprang to action and led me toward the curtain with the white-coated man on my heels. She explained that I needed to have my eyes examined; then the lenses could be cut and ready for my new frames in ten days or so. Soon I was face-to-face with Albert, who stood to clear the small hallway leading to the examination room. I gave him what I hoped was a friendly smile. He shot me a look of confusion, but still there was the smallest hint of a timid smile. As the doctor led me away into the examination room, I contemplated my next move. Should I introduce myself and quickly tell him that I wanted to talk to him? Should I just give him my phone number, knowing that I would look strange and pushy? Should I act like I knew him from the University and ask him to meet for a coffee after work? None of these options appealed to me. The last one was the worst of the three possibilities and the first one was clearly the most aggressive.

After my examination, I was swept back to the front of the store before I could even look at Albert again. I gave the clerk my contact details and set up an appointment to return for the glasses. I could have waited, I suppose, to talk to Albert the following week, but I was not going to leave anything to chance. I tore a page out of my notebook and wrote down my name and phone number on it. The saleswoman looked on, curious. "Excuse me," I said, turning away from her and heading back toward the green curtain.

Albert was back in his chair with his shoulders hunched toward each other. I didn't bother for him to look up; I just acted before I lost my resolve. I held out a piece of paper. "Please," I said firmly, trying not to show my desperation, "this is my number. Call me. It is important." I knew I was being more than a little melodramatic. Albert didn't reach for the paper; instead, he stared at me with amused horror. "Really, I'm serious. Please." If he had waited a moment longer, my confidence would have slipped and I imagine I would have succumbed to begging. He took the paper with great reluctance. I left the store as quickly as I could, hoping I hadn't scared him off.

EVEN UNDER THE BEST of circumstances, it is ridiculous for someone to wait by the phone for it to ring, but I did so anyway. I waited and waited until it was nearly time for me to head back to the shop to collect my glasses. When Albert finally did call one evening, he made it clear right off that he thought this was all a big joke.

"Did Gigi set you up to this?" he asked.

"No, let me explain," I said.

"C'mon, I know he's behind this. Listen, thanks, but—"

I interrupted, "I don't know anyone named Gigi, I promise. I wanted to speak to you about your mother."

I heard a sharp intake of breath. It wasn't shock but something else: the vocal equivalent of a slingshot being drawn back. I waited in silence, not sure what to expect next.

"What the . . . what the fuck are you talking about?" Albert shouted into the phone. Words, brutal and angry, poured from his mouth as if years of pent-up frustration at his mother had finally found the escape hatch. Under this siege of hostility I tried to explain, but he was beyond reason. "No, no, no! Don't you fucking speak to me! Who are you? Some whore who acts as her fucking mouthpiece? I don't want anything to do with her!"

I realized that I was shaking with anger, more upset that he was so irrational and so incapable of hearing my explanation. I started shouting into the phone: "Listen to me! Listen to me! Will you just shut up and listen to me?" But I knew it was too late. He had already slammed down the phone.

I smashed the phone into its cradle and stood in my darkened hallway, fuming.

"Everything all right?" My flatmate stuck her head out of her bedroom door.

"Just beautiful." I said, without turning to face her.

CHAPTER 15.
Changes

MOST PEOPLE KNOW THE moment their life changes forever, and Pauline was no different. It was early April. The spring rains were just cold enough to keep her in the tiny apartment. Pauline hated being trapped inside, but she hated being cold even more. Her sister Joyce was out with the children; Albert was eleven, and her daughter, Isabel, was three. The morning had dragged on in its usual way, with Albert away at school and Pauline trying to escape the demands of her daughter, who annoyed her with her constant crying. The child always seemed to be hurting herself, bumping into walls, slamming her fingers in a cabinet, stubbing her toe on pieces of furniture, and falling down. Being around her daughter rattled Pauline's nerves; sometimes she would lose her self-control and give Isabel a kick or a shake or smack her on the bum.

NOW THAT THE FLAT was silent, she was alone and bored. Charles was at the university, probably at the library, but she couldn't say for sure. Charles was always away from early morning until just about dinnertime. He would come home and play with the children, eat, take a shower, and then sit at the dining room table with his books. He did this every day except Saturdays and Sundays. On Saturdays he would wake up early, and he and Albert would go out in shorts or track pants and sneakers. Pauline guessed that they went to play football; they returned in the late evening, well past dinnertime. And Sundays the whole family acted like they were Italian and window-shopped or walked in the park, the five of them eagerly lapping gelati from a cone.

Pauline eventually stopped attending these Sunday outings. Not too long before, one Sunday when Pauline, Joyce, Charles, and the two kids had been standing in front of a display window outside the department store La Rinascente, Pauline had caught the sight of them reflected in the window. She could remember seeing them as the rest of the world did. "To others, we must have looked like those Africans who just washed ashore—in awe of the wealth of Europe and ready to beg for a piece of it." Soon, no outing was innocent; Pauline looked for signs of their lesser status in the faces of the people she passed.

She recognized that this was a futile exercise. Pauline could handle the obvious racism, the nasty comments, and the angry stares. She was fine with all of that. She expected it. But one of the things she hated most about living in Italy was the *perception* that people looked down on her because she was African, foreign, supposedly poor, and uneducated. And it was that specific—Pauline despised being lumped in with every other African, because she had always felt that she was different, special, a person who could change things. "I grew up thinking that my name would go down in history."

But living in Rome changed her mind. With each passing day, Pauline feared that she might not amount to anything. This feeling of uncertainty was new to her; in fact, even after several years of living in Europe, everything still felt new to her. Though she had lived among white people before, it was not like this. She wasn't shocked or impressed by them, the way others were, but she sometimes grew tired of "being around all that difference."

That was what pushed her to find people who seemed similar to her. She set off in search of other Africans. "I wanted to find someone from Kampala, a man or a woman—it didn't matter. I just wanted someone who could share a *waragi* [a common Ugandan distilled alcohol] with me."

Pauline found Dora, a tall Kenyan girl who ran a hair salon out of her apartment near the train station. Pauline admired Dora's life, mainly her freedom and the fact that she was a self-made woman. Pauline quickly adapted to life at Dora's place. But still, they were different. Dora had her own money and entertained men, she set her own working hours, she traveled when she wanted and stayed out late if the mood struck. Though Pauline left the children with her sister and Charles and spent most of her time over at Dora's, she never spent the night; she still liked the feel of her own bed and didn't want to listen to any sounds except the ones she made. And out of respect for her friend, Pauline wanted to give Dora the chance to have a man over if she wanted to, so she never went over too early, especially when she discovered that Dora was dating a Nigerian guy who called himself "Thank God."

Thank God was tall and lanky and always wore a suit. Pauline thought he talked too much nonsense. He was always going on about wanting babies and being in love with Dora. "He was like a woman with all that carrying on," Pauline told me. But she had started to quietly observe more and more about Thank God, like who he spent his time with and how he got his money.

She had seen him with a few white men—Italians, she thought—for whom she believed he sold drugs. He was always coming and going with them. Then one day Thank God brought one of the white men over to Dora's. He introduced Besnik from Albania briefly before the two men sat at the small kitchen table and pulled out papers in preparation to smoke some hash. Pauline watched from a corner in the kitchen, amused at Thank God's shaking hands and obvious nervousness. She couldn't stop herself from making a joke: "Looks like Thank God could use a little help. Maybe I should get a priest?"

Bresnik looked up and smiled at her, not laughing but appreciating her attempt at humor. That was all it took. Pauline accepted his smile like an invitation to the world. Her mind was already busy scheming about the journey ahead. But she knew she had to pace herself.

CHAPTER 16.
Drug Orphan

I WAS NOT PREPARED for Albert to be so caustic. But I knew I would keep trying—we just had too much in common. We were nearly the same age. We were university students. Both of his parents had been sent to prison; so had mine. And apparently, neither one of us could forgive them for that.

Clearly, more than some of Albert's mother had rubbed off on him. And then I immediately thought of my own mother—whom at that moment I pictured sitting on her sofa in California, reading a book. Was my mother as much a part of me as Pauline was of Albert? Like Albert, had I tried and failed to exorcise the very person I resembled most? I never allowed myself to think that I was anything like my mother, and I wasn't ready to start doing that now—not yet.

Perhaps years ago I would have been able to forge connections between Pauline and my mom, just enough to damn the both of them in my mind. But my mother was very different from Pauline: softer, less sure of herself. The truth was that Pauline reminded me of my father, or what I imagined my father to be. He was the parent whom I had always been most interested in, and being in Rebibbia and talking to people who smuggled drugs seemed to make him more alive to me. He haunted me throughout my time in Rome. He was everywhere.

I thought too much of my parents these days. I supposed it was inevitable. Given their history with imprisonment, I expected that my time at Rebibbia would start to bring up memories from my childhood. I had prepared myself for the eerie walks down long and noisy institutional corridors. The barbed wire, guard towers, and barred windows seemed to come straight out of the nightmares of my youth.

It was also inevitable that I would think about my mother. I knew that being in a women's prison, hearing the stories of women who, like her, had fallen down the rabbit hole of difficult circumstances compounded by very bad decisions, would deliver me right back to the feelings of confusion and longing that had marked my formative years. Prison had orphaned me, even after my mother came home. Perhaps it did so especially because my father never did.

My dad, David Lamont Jenkins, ran one of the largest heroin operations in Riverside County, just outside Los Angeles, until the early 1970s. Since I never met my father, everything I knew about him I learned from the unsatisfying accounts my mother told me, the rumors my grandmother started, and a private investigator's incomplete report.

When I returned home from the prison one afternoon, I phoned my mother. "Why are you calling?" she asked. The question was typical of her; she may have been excited to speak to me, her faraway daughter whom she hadn't seen in more than a year, but she would never show it. I had forgotten how stern she could be. Frankly, I wasn't sure why I had called. But I wanted to talk.

"Tell me about my dad." My oft-repeated request had a mixed record of being granted. I waited.

"Your dad looked exactly like a young Isaac Hayes," she finally said, in a tone that implied that she had told me this a thousand times already. But this was new information to me. I tried to picture Isaac Hayes as my father; the round-faced, bald-headed, older Isaac near the end of his life came to mind—not even close to looking like my dad, I was sure.

I had seen my father once, in a photograph. It was the only photo of my parents together, taken by my grandmother on the street outside her home when my folks were merely dating. My mother, who was eighteen years old, was standing with her arms crossed over her stomach, wearing a shapeless brown shirt and jeans. She was barefoot. Her hair hung in thin brown strings past her shoulders; her eyes were tiny slits behind her thick glasses. She was sandwiched between two black men. One was tall and very handsome, wearing a brown vest and tight, striped bell-bottoms; the other was short, his eyes also squinting toward the sun, wearing a dark blue suit, a crisp white shirt, and a green tie.

My father, who was nineteen, was not in the habit of wearing a suit. He was on his way to an interview for a job that he would not get. It was clear that my grandmother had forced the photo shoot on the teenagers. I was not surprised by the look of indifference on my mother's face.

My parents married shortly after the photo was taken. Their union was brief and mostly unhappy. I have never received a clear answer about how long they were together, but three years sounds about right. My grandmother was fond of telling my sister and me about how, just an hour after my mother eloped, she called from Tijuana, sobbing. It was like a scene from a bad after-school special: My mother said that she had ruined her life—she was pregnant. That she would end up with twins, or "twofers," was a lesson in Murphy's law.

My mother managed to suck up her remorse upon her return from Mexico. It helped that my father would end up missing much of her pregnancy because he was busy being a fugitive in Canada. However, the weeks my parents did live together were not without incident. Apparently, they had more than a few arguments about their lifestyle. David was a heroin addict, but my mother was less interested in getting my father to stop taking drugs than she was in making him stop selling them.

This was particularly true a month following my birth, when police and agents from the Bureau of Narcotics and Dangerous Drugs, the agency that begat the Drug Enforcement

Administration, searched my parents' home—"everywhere but your crib," my mother told me over the phone. But David was lucky that time. The house was clean, his whereabouts unknown—as was typical, he had been gone on a five- or six-day binge. The police asked my mother a few questions and then let her go, but not before the fear of prison had become cemented in her mind.

My dad was a different sort of trafficker than Pauline, though they both moved heroin across borders. The heroin trade in California in the 1960s and early 1970s looked far different from the way it currently does. At the peak of my father's business, he sold to about one hundred people a day, according to an estimate from the neighbor who reported my parents to the police, and was running a full-service operation. My dad's clients would hand over a few bucks to him or to my mother in exchange for a little bag of drugs that could be inhaled, smoked, or, most frequently, injected. People shot up right in my parents' living room.

The heroin that people freebased at the house was called black tar and brown powder—both types came from Mexico. "Chiva" was widely used in the West Coast drug scene back then. My dad smuggled his drugs across the border, usually driving them up Interstate 5 by himself. Sometimes he would collect heroin from suppliers in Canada or other U.S. cities as well. This other heroin—white powder that was sourced in central and Southeast Asia—was usually brought into the United States by the Corsican networks, also known as the French Connection, who were based in Marseilles. The European heroin was the drug of choice on the East Coast of the United States and would have been a little bit more expensive for my father to get a hold of. But when he did, it must have been a real boon, as the purity could have been up to 85 percent and it was far easier to cut for profitable resale on the streets than the Mexican chiva was.

As far as I know, my father did not work for anyone but himself. He had a few employees, friends mainly, who were paid in drugs. And then there was my mother, who wasn't paid at all. Perhaps she didn't need to be paid; I have often suspected that she was a silent partner in my dad's operation. She was adept at recruiting her female friends to buy as much lactose as the local grocery stores would allow. She knew that the lactose, cooked and uncooked, was the perfect cutting agent for any kind of heroin. It increased the bulk of the drugs and made heroin easier to inhale.

Beyond chemistry, Mom also knew the exact moment when she and my dad needed to ditch an apartment—usually after a few months, when the loitering junkies became too obvious to hide. Of course, this would be just about the time when rent was due. And since moving vans brought too much unwanted attention, my mother would pack a couple of plastic garbage bags full of clothes and leave everything else behind. I suspect that she relied on dope fiends to move her. Usually, anything of value would eventually find its way back to my parents, as addicts, having broken into our family's unoccupied home, would barter our furniture for their drugs.

My father was part of a small, decentralized network of traffickers who pieced their businesses together on the west coast.

The French Connection and the CIA, who allegedly trafficked heroin in the 1970s, were the biggest players in the "smack" trade. Without the ethos of the notoriously brutal Colombian cartels that would emerge a few years later, and lacking the weaponry of today's Mexican paramilitary-like drug operations, my dad's era offered enough room for anyone who was interested in selling drugs to be involved.

"We might have been a bunch of hippies, but it wasn't all innocent," my mother told me. "I mean, it's not like we were like Scarface or anything. But we had guns in the house and we used them." She did not sound at all apologetic.

MY DAD STARTED DEALING heroin at the start of the American fascination with recreational drug use. In 1960, getting high was still something that people on the fringes of society did. But by 1975, it had moved from the counterculture to the mainstream, fast on its way to becoming the unavoidable fact of life that it is today. From the time I started grade school in the late 1970s, the wave of moral panic around drugs would ebb and flow with greater degrees of intensity well into my adulthood. I have come to see the decades of my life through the lens of various antidrug campaigns, from the PREVENT DRUG ABUSE postage stamps of the 1970s, the "Just Say No" slogan of the 1980s, and the 1990s taglines "This is your brain. This is your brain on drugs" and "Winners Don't Use Drugs" to the more contractual arrangement of the 2000s: the "say no to drugs and yes to life drug-free" pledge.

As a child, I had no concept of the fact that my dad played an instrumental role in destroying not only his life, but also the lives of others. My father's absence allowed me to turn him into whatever I wanted him to be. Ultimately, I reasoned, it didn't matter what anyone said about him, whether they called him a criminal, a womanizer, a violent man, or a drug addict. In my mind, my father was compassionate, fair, and deeply misunderstood. What I didn't know was that I would not grow out of this sentiment until I finally met my father's doppelgänger, or at least what I imagined was a close approximation of him, in Pauline.

CHAPTER 17.

Monrovia Bound

THE DAY AFTER SHE heard the news about the orphanage, Mary left the refuge of the school. With Peter and Jacob in tow, she headed south toward Grand Gedeh County, her heart filled with the hope of seeing her daughter again, alive.

But Mary was unlucky. She spent weeks trying to find the orphanage, and when she finally came upon it, nothing about the place resembled even slightly what the crazy woman had described.

"There were no foreigners, no food for the handful of tired-looking children, and the place looked like it had been sacked so many times by crooks that even I was embarrassed by my 'rich' appearance," Mary recalled to me. She called out to a boy of about ten to ask him if Catherine was among the children. When he said no, she didn't even bother to stop to have a look around herself. She continued walking.

Mary finally made the decision to get as far away from Liberia as possible, but first she had to go back to Monrovia. There she discovered that she now had to share her house with the extended family of her groundskeeper. They had squatted in every room and filled the place with trash, chickens, and crying children. Her house had long been in disarray, but the mess and destruction weren't what she minded so much. It was actually better this way, Mary thought: If her house were still the way it had before she'd left, it would mean there was a small possibility that she could pretend to lead a normal life now. This way, with the house looking like it belonged to someone else, it was easier for her to accept all that had been taken from her. But when she stood in the room that had once belonged to her and James, she let herself cry, not for his death and not for the memories, but for how much she had loved him.

Mary left the house and picked her way through streets crowded with rusted cars, people from the villages, soldiers from Nigeria. She headed for James's old office, not knowing what she should expect to find. When she got there, the place looked almost the same: two small desks, a map of Africa on the wall, and a painted sign that announced the name of the company. James and his partner, David, had never hung it because of the spelling mistake that they had caught after they paid the painter, who had already left for the day.

David was sitting at his desk. He and Mary were both surprised to see each other. They had both changed in appearance, but they ignored this fact to talk about the changes their lives had taken.

"James was killed" was all Mary could say to him.

"AFL?" he asked, understanding that no other words needed to be exchanged about the matter.

Mary shook her head. She had reached a place in her mind where it didn't matter who had killed James. The war had killed him. Foolish cowards had killed him. Her own complicity, and David's too, had killed him. She had left Monrovia and felt like she had seen her country for what it was: animals leading humans to their slaughter. Between Doe's men, Taylor's men, and Johnson's men, Mary realized that it was only a matter of time before someone got to her and her family.

David must have realized this, too, for he had taken his wife and daughters to be registered by the United Nations at a nearby office so that they could be sent to a refugee camp in a neighboring country.

"What about you?" Mary asked.

David shrugged his shoulders. "I am not ready to go. Soon, but not yet."

She understood his feelings. She was torn between her own nihilism and her obligations as a mother. Catherine was out there somewhere and Mary needed to find her. Her sons were going hungry. She feared that all of her children had seen too much of death to ever have a normal childhood.

David took Mary to a foreign-aid office where the lines were long and the aid workers, some African and some white, seemed impatient and worried. As Mary spoke to a white woman—German or French; she could not tell by her accent—she became aware that the woman before her had heard stories like Mary's a thousand times, so there was no use giving complete answers to her emotionless questions.

"We were two shells speaking to each other. I wasn't there and she wasn't there," Mary said. "The more I talked, the more I could see that she didn't care—I mean, she didn't care in her heart. To her, I was going to be another number in a report that she would file to receive more money to hand out bags of rice. I was grateful, yes, but I had heard the promises that they had made to people who came before me in line. I couldn't wait for their help."

Refusing to continue with her pointless interview, Mary asked David to take her to the first of many "trapping centers," as she called them. The first center was neither an official orphanage nor a tracing center for lost children. It seemed to be a school that housed mostly young boys to keep them away from the war. But in the days that followed, as Mary continued her search for Catherine and found no sign of her at any of the agencies in Monrovia, she registered as a refugee and waited to be told where she would be sent.

CHAPTER 18.
A Business of Virtues

IT DIDN'T TAKE BRESNIK long to bring Pauline into the fold. After a few months of strategically placing herself in his way, getting rid of that house servant, that "Gishu boy," Thank God, and arranging for Dora to be Bresnik's lover, Pauline had become trustworthy enough to hold on to a few things for him: a little bit of money at first, then dope, and then both in higher quantities.

Bresnik started taking her places. Once, they drove through Rome until the city streets led to highways that bled out to small, tree-lined roads and fields. But mostly they stayed around the city, stopping off at cafés, restaurants, an auto-re-pair shop, a couple of nightclubs, and a bakery that opened only at night.

At first Pauline stayed in the car while Bresnik went inside. When she did get out of the car, the other men would look at her briefly and one might ask, "Who's she?" To which Bresnik would say, "A friend." Everyone would then turn to appraise her; Pauline would notice the looks of curiosity and amusement they gave off. Bresnik would come to his own rescue, laughing at an unspoken joke: "No way, my girl is at home; Zeno is just a friend. Right, Z? She's my bulldog, my protection against you assholes."

Pauline was never offended. She was never interested in Bresnik. She supposed he was attractive, but not as handsome as he thought he was. Everything about Bresnik was proportionate except his long black hair, which he wore loose and past his shoulders. After his little jokes about her being a bulldog or protector, Pauline would watch silently as all the men laughed uproariously, slapping each other's backs, reinforcing their manhood.

But it was true: Pauline did protect Bresnik. And soon enough, these men would come to know it through rumors on the street or through eyewitness accounts. Pauline was waiting for the opportunity to prove herself, and it came one evening when she and Bresnik went to collect some money at an auto-repair garage.

Even before she got out of the car, Pauline saw a man pacing the floor in short, angry steps. "This guy wants a fight," she told Bresnik. Sure enough, the agitated man stepped forward and began shouting at them. He held up his fists to Bresnik, but Pauline didn't let him get too close. She told me,

"I picked up one of those long things that you wash windows with [a squeegee] and beat that man with the flat rubber side until it snapped and flew into the air. When I got him to his knees, I kicked his penis as hard as I could."

Pauline walked away from the fight with men staring at her in stunned silence. When she and Bresnik reached the car, he said, "I didn't know you could do that." Pauline shrugged and said, "Next time, listen to me."

SOON SHE WAS PROTECTING Bresnik in other ways. She told him who to look out for and who to trust. Bresnik was ambitious but not nearly as much as she was, so she helped him as a way of helping herself. "He had a very narrow view of what was out there for him, the possibilities. I could see it all—everything that I wanted and how I was going to get there," she said. And for a while, at least, Pauline needed Bresnik.

Pauline called him an "easy pick" because she knew from the first moment that she met him what he could offer her. She was always good at reading people. It was a skill that she had learned from her uncle Kefa, who used to brag about fighting alongside Idi Amin against the Mau Maus back in 1952. When Pauline was a child, he had taken her out to the market in Kampala and made her watch the lives of the people before them. They had returned day after day until Pauline knew who the market people were and how they acted in various situations. Uncle Kefa would translate their gestures and anticipate what they'd do next.

As she got older, he would tell her about "personality types," and how to determine a person's secret wishes or desires. He taught her a great many things, but he didn't teach her about the extra-special power that she would have because she was a woman. As she described it, "People, men especially, want to trust women; they need to. From a girl to a woman, people would tell me things about them without my having to ask too much." Because men thought women were weak, Pauline once explained, they showed sides of themselves that other men rarely saw. In her mind, it helped that she was no beauty queen—she didn't have to worry about things getting sexual.

Pauline knew that Bresnik was just a stop along the way to something bigger. She had no intention of making her impact on the world by hanging around a midlevel operator. Bresnik worked on the distribution side of the drug business. His crew moved marijuana, hash, and a little bit of cocaine to buyers who would sell it in smaller quantities in clubs or on the streets. While he never touched the drugs himself, Bresnik did handle the money. His job was collecting cash after the deliveries.

Pauline found this curious; it was like giving something away for free. She pushed him to appeal to his boss about doing it another way. But Bresnik wasn't so sure; this was before the Albanians formed strong gangs amongst themselves, so he, like many other Eastern European guys, worked for the Italians. The Italian couple Bresnik worked for had always done business this way, collecting the money after the drugs had been delivered. "It kept them small," Pauline said, "and I hated being small."

Without capital in advance of a drug purchase, there were never any guarantees that deliveries would be made on time or ever. In Pauline's mind, it was bad business. She grew frustrated. It wasn't about the money for her, though she earned very little when she worked for Bresnik. She wanted to set her sights higher.

The business of smuggling drugs is like any enterprise in which innovation, speed, and anticipation are key to survival. No two smuggling rings are alike, but there are some similarities between syndicates. Since the late 1980s, starting with the fall of the Medellín Cartel in Colombia, the drug-smuggling business has transformed itself into a boutique operation. This is not to say that there are no longer cartels—large, complex organizations that grow, process, transport, and distribute their own drugs—because there are. But for most international smuggling rings, everyone fills a niche. It's a pyramid scheme within a pyramid scheme. There are people who supply only the drugs, usually uncut and sold directly from the farm or farms that produce them. Then there is a broker—and this job is just what it sounds like. Sometimes brokers can be part of a very long chain that blends the roles of supplier and broker. But mostly, brokers make contact with the buyers and arrange for the drugs to be sent.

That's where transporters come in. They have the job of getting the drugs from one place to another, usually across several different borders; therefore, there is often (but not always) more than one crew that transports. Once the drugs get into the buyers' hands, there is usually a whole other level of supplying, brokering, transporting, and distributing that takes place. The more steps a crew takes to fulfill each role, the more money it stands to make, but the greater danger it faces.

Pauline never asked herself if she would have chosen any other line of work. She chose drug trafficking and she liked it. She once said, "This is a business of strong virtues; it's about respect, strength, loyalty, and dedication. There are no long lunches, no buggering off before 5:00 PM, no sick calls. Everyone doing this is doing it because they like it: the pace, the risk, the money, the lifestyle. Everyone. From the lowest person to the highest." In Pauline's mind, there was little difference between the products she sold and cigarette companies like Philip Morris. "They make money off of people's weakness, and so do we."

CHAPTER 19.

All Our Kin

"WE WERE BAREFOOT, YOU know." Mary was sitting across from me in the prison. Her memories lay between us. When she spoke, it was as if I were not there. She was very still. Her hands rested on thick, round thighs mocking the size of the plastic chair. Her legs were encased in black spandex leggings ending several inches above her ankles. The flesh there puffed and pillowed under the pressure of the tight elastic. Dull red toenails peeked out from old black sandals. Her heels hung suspended off the back of them. The ill-fitting clothes did nothing to hide Mary's stature. Her weariness seemed embedded in her skin, the kind of exhaustion that time could never take away. Mary's bloodshot eyes were deep, glistening black pools. They were the kind of eyes that look inward.

"Some path to prison, huh?" Her voice was calm. I took her in with a full stare, one that tried to chronicle her existence. Her hair was short, but she pulled it back in the tightest, smallest bun I had ever seen. Small bald patches were starting to form near her temples. Her skin was bad. But underneath this broken-down veneer, Mary was a woman who looked like she knew how to get things done.

Almost embarrassed, the corners of her mouth flipped quickly into a smile and then flatlined. It was the first real sign of life to sneak across her face. I stared at her shirt, blurring the multicolored flowers against their black background until the colors seem to swirl together. I searched for something to say.

Not long after our first meeting, Mary said, "You know that my name is Johnson. Do you know that name, Johnson?" I looked at her for a moment, uncertain where she was going. Johnson is a common surname in Liberia.

Her eyes stared into mine intently. "You know Prince Johnson?"

I sat up straight. I knew about Prince Johnson.

"He is a relative."

I nodded, understanding why she would not say any more.

A former training officer in Charles Taylor's NPFL, the "Prince," as he named himself, broke off and formed his own faction, the Independent National Patriotic Front of Liberia (INPFL). In September 1990, Prince Johnson made world headlines when he kidnapped president Samuel Doe and then videotaped his torture and murder. Set to a musical score, the tape *INPFL Forever* showed a sweaty Johnson sitting behind a large desk with a garland of hand grenades around his neck, a beer in his hand, and a young woman dabbing his brow. Surrounded by his men, Johnson pounded the desk, shouting at Doe, "Where's the money you took from the Liberian people?" Doe was writhing on the floor, his face and body glistening with sweat and blood. "That man won't talk! Bring me his ear!" The camera focused in on a screaming Doe as drunken rebels held him down and sliced off his left ear and then, later, his right.

Mary Johnson was neither proud of nor anguished by her family tree. She knew that her husband, his brothers and sisters, and their children were killed because they were related to Johnson.

"The war was still new then," she told me. I knew that wasn't an apology for Johnson. "We still thought of ourselves as transitioning, as if at any moment the country could change its mind and go back to more peaceful times. It never happened." She turned her face up to the prison windows. There was nothing to see outside except gray. After a moment, she explained that in the early period of the conflict, she and her husband never considered themselves "political." In fact, Mary told me, they hardly knew Prince Johnson.

When fighting first broke out in Monrovia, people seemed to turn in on themselves, full of unspoken fear. It was as if life stood still. All people could do was either watch or join in the feast. "And so," Mary said, "we walked. And we kept walking, sleeping on the sides of roads, sleeping where we could. Sometimes we would leave one area that was fighting, only to be in the middle of it in the next. It took us four months, but finally we got out of the country.

"I got a ride over the border to the Ivory Coast. But they didn't want Liberians; there were too many of us. There are pieces of my dignity still on those roads out there, and I cannot bring myself to tell you what that journey cost me. But everything I did, everything I have done, has been for my sons. I stayed alive for them." She sat with her hands folded on her lap.

Mary leaned forward to see what I was writing and said, "My children mean everything to me—write that down."

CHAPTER 20.
Meeting Emmanuel

PAULINE COULD TAKE BRESNIK'S small dealing world for only so long. After more than a year of working for him, she was ready to move on. As usual, she kept her eyes open for opportunities, and eventually one came, when she became infatuated with a man named Emmanuel.

Pauline first met him in Spain when she was there with Bresnik on a drug buy for the Italians. She was at a small African restaurant in Barcelona. It was late in the afternoon and the place was empty—most customers would not be in until later that evening. Pauline noticed Emmanuel sitting off by himself, clearly an outsider in the dingy place. She felt his eyes on her as she, Bresnik, and the Spanish contact, a Nigerian man called Jojo, sat down for beers at a small table.

She noticed Emmanuel for two reasons. First, because she usually hated to see men wear jewelry, and he wore a gold bracelet. But it went so beautifully with his outfit—matching cream-colored linen trousers and shirt, both loose-fitting and flowing, and brown loafers—that she could not resist admiring him. And second, she had seen the way his eyes had lit up into flashing, disturbed question marks when she had entered the room. That he had even acknowledged Pauline was surprising to her.

She knew better than to flatter herself. It wasn't that he was handsome—Pauline thought his looks were average. But Emmanuel was special somehow, different. He was gentle, but not soft. Pauline watched as he leaned his large frame over the bar. He was like a sponge absorbing their conversation, studying it. Though he tried to appear as if he were not part of the meeting that was about to take place, Pauline knew otherwise. She tested her theory by speaking to Jojo loud enough for Emmanuel to hear: "Will your friend join us, or is he here to pour our drinks?"

Emmanuel stretched up slowly and grabbed three glasses with one hand and two large bottles of beer in the other. Without any humor, he put the bottle and glasses on the table and said softly, "I own this place. If you want to stay in it, don't talk too much." It was the first time Pauline felt something move within her when someone spoke. She sat uncharacteristically quiet throughout much of the meeting, not sure if she wanted to please Emmanuel or if she was too afraid to defy him.

Before they left for Italy the next day, she went back to the restaurant to look for him. It was early, but he was there, sipping coffee while listening intently to the BBC World Service. He didn't seem shocked to see her and asked if she wanted a coffee. She shook her head and sat down next to him. She was close enough to touch him. She wasn't sure how she was going to make her proposal, but she knew she had to do it at that moment or the opportunity would be lost.

Nervousness was new to Pauline, but so much of what she had felt over the last twelve hours since meeting him was new to her. She had stayed up all night, not even trying to pretend to sleep. She had drafted plan after plan and rehearsed every line, but now it sounded too clever and she just wanted to be sincere. She worked her nerve up slowly, feeling Emmanuel's patience turn edgy.

"So?" he asked.

"So, I was thinking that I should stay here for a while. I could stay in Spain and help you run things."

"What makes you think I need an assistant?"

Pauline scrambled to make herself clear, but she didn't even know what she was asking for just yet. "No, no, not like that. I know you don't need an assistant, but you could use someone like me. "

Pauline was feeling desperate. Her proposal had evaporated, and now she was spilling out something that sounded more like a disorganized plea. Before Emmanuel could brush her off, she tried again. What she had concluded the day before was that Emmanuel was more than a restaurateur. It was obvious. Jojo was his front man, the man who got his hands dirty meeting with the likes of her and her Albanian mate. She knew that he was a broker in this business, but she also knew that there had to be more. Pauline wanted in, so she told him something that she had kept from everyone.

Her husband, Charles, had a cousin who worked for the Ugandan government in the Ministry of Foreign Affairs. He had financed their move to Rome and was the reason why Charles had received a state-sponsored fellowship to study in Italy. Pauline trusted Cousin Henry; she knew he was a man of few scruples, so she went to him with all of her concerns about working for the *bazungu* (white) drug dealers. She wanted Henry's help in setting up her own operation, which meant that she needed money and some contacts. Henry had agreed, but only in exchange for more than a 50 percent partnership in the venture. Pauline wasn't worried about that—she had secured the money that she needed and "would have no trouble cutting Henry out" when she needed to.

Emmanuel listened intently, and when she was finished explaining that her ultimate goal was to open new routes through Africa using commercial shipping lines to eastern Europe, he laughed.

"What makes you think that those routes are not already there?" he asked.

Pauline said with confidence, "If you think that you could do better than me with that thick-neck Jojo, then stick with him. But I know better."

"Jojo may be a little dim, that's true," Emmanuel laughed, "but I have known him since we had milk teeth."

"Oh, please, that doesn't mean that you can't know me." Pauline countered.

"All right, let's say that I know you."

Pauline was in, sort of. It would take another six months to convince him, but she had found her way to a new partnership, and it was all the better that it came in the form of Emmanuel.

CHAPTER 21.
Educating Pauline

PAULINE HATED LIVING IN Barcelona. The streets were too wide, the city moved too slowly. It lacked the energy of Kampala or Rome. For Pauline, Barcelona was like a village. And like a village, it seemed to hold its breath, waiting for something exciting to occur. But nothing ever did.

Emmanuel had given Pauline an apartment. It was a small, dreary place with walls that looked as if someone had cleaned them with a muddy rag. The floors were oily and grimy. The overall effect was depressing. Pauline recalled, "I had left a basic student flat in Rome to move into something that was no better than a doghouse. I knew better than to complain too much about anything—Emmanuel liked to test my limits, you see—but that? Oh, no, I made sure that he knew how I felt."

Within three weeks, Emmanuel moved Pauline to his house outside Barcelona. It was an improvement, but still

Pauline was not happy. Emmanuel and his crew lived and worked in the city, and she was too far away from the action, so, as usual, she took matters into her own hands and moved into a rented room that she shared with "another African girl, a French speaker." Pauline never really knew her name.

Pauline's life was different for the first time in years. "You know," she said, "I don't worry about doing what I want. And in Spain, I started over, all by myself, without obligations. Do you know what it feels like to have a chance to start over? Not only to start over, but to be putting your mind to something, chasing down opportunities, knowing that if you fail, you fail alone, if you succeed, you did it all on your own—there is nothing like that feeling." She didn't have a problem with the fact that she was going deeper into the drug business. "I choose this business because it suited me."

Though Pauline had already been working for a couple of years in the drug trade, she saw herself as an apprentice for a midlevel, a lower-midlevel, operator. When she met Emmanuel, she learned enough to know what was possible—mainly, the money that could be made—if one could reach just a little higher.

It didn't take Pauline long to depart Rome. It was just a few days after she returned from her initial trip to Spain, when she had proposed to Emmanuel that they go into business together. She had no qualms about leaving Charles with the children. Looking back, Pauline was not sure if she had even said goodbye to them. But it didn't matter, because she knew that she would not be in Spain for too long. Or so she thought.

At first, Emmanuel had Pauline running around like a secretary. She said nothing, even though she quickly grew bored of the tasks she had to perform. Emmanuel had her managing some of his legitimate businesses—for example, doing the books for his restaurant and filling out shipping forms for the oil company he owned in Nigeria. In this way, he kept her close but out of the way of his drug business. She understood. He was protecting himself. If she were him, she thought, she would do the same. But after a few months, Pauline began to wonder if Emmanuel liked her too much in the role he had given her. She decided that she needed to take some action.

Her plan was to gradually move into the "money-making side" of his business. If Emmanuel wanted to keep an eye on her, she needed more visibility. She had to be everywhere he was. Pauline wanted to be a true business partner, but she needed to create some distance between her and the rest of the people around him. True, she was enamored with him—that was obvious—but Emmanuel never exploited her feelings for him, at least not at that stage.

Pauline didn't try to be subtle. She made arrangements for a visit to Uganda. She boldly booked a flight for herself, Emmanuel, and Jojo, whose function was to never leave Emmanuel's side. She set up meetings with what she called the "investors" and even contacted a tourist agency to schedule a sightseeing trip of Kampala for Emmanuel. She reasoned, "I wanted him to see that I was a businesswoman, that I was serious and so were my investors. Uganda was open for business. I couldn't overlook anything."

It was a simple plan, but it had taken months to arrive at this moment. Pauline waited until she thought she would have the best chance to get a positive reaction from Emmanuel. He hated surprises and especially hated being pressured to do anything, but Pauline was desperate. It was now, or she was going to have to walk away, and she didn't want that—not yet. But too much time had been wasted. She and Emmanuel were strictly friendly with each other; the fact that she was attracted to him did not, could not, cloud her judgment. She needed a business partner. She wanted him to fill the role.

She knew that he would act annoyed when she handed over the tickets, but the truth, as Pauline had seen the first day she had met Emmanuel, was that he needed her. The more time she spent around Emmanuel and the restaurant, the more she understood that his drug operation was a loosely configured free-for-all. Pauline remembered, "Emmanuel had gone into this when anyone could walk into the trade with three dollars and come out the other side with three million. He was like a lot of people in those times: He started with a little cash, bought a kilogram or so of cocaine or H [heroin], put it in a bag, carried it back to Spain, where he sold it for a profit. And that was the birth of his business. The problem was, ten years later, he was still running it like that, but with fifty or sixty Emmanuels, not the one, it was getting out of control."

The worst part of it was that Emmanuel was losing money. Originally, he had had suppliers who got their heroin from Burma, but they had started to routinely miss shipments through seizure or pirating, leaving him seeking other sources. So he had turned to Afghanistan, where the prices were higher, and to Pakistan, where trafficking routes were new to him and therefore more costly. But the roads from those countries to Europe in the mid- to late 1980s were well worn, so he paid the money but didn't like the exposure.

Out of necessity, he brought more people on and shipped cut and uncut heroin through various parts of Africa, making use of the lack of security controls at docks and airports. Emmanuel was not a pioneer in this regard. In the late 1980s and early '90s, it seemed that all of Africa was on the radar for many smuggling operations but ignored almost completely by police and international crime-fighting officials.

By the time Pauline came to him, in the early 1990s, Emmanuel had narrowed his routes in and out of Africa to Nigeria, and the cocaine and heroin markets that he traded in were becoming saturated worldwide.

Prices were falling slightly, but consumption was still on the rise, and more and more criminal networks did what any business would do—they expanded. They took more risks. Trafficking out of Afghanistan and Pakistan didn't last long for Emmanuel, despite the fact that around this time, as reported by the United Nations, African criminal groups, mainly Nigerians, got more involved with heroin smuggling from Golden Crescent countries through Pakistan and India. The Pakistani city of Karachi was the main port for heroin brought in from the Pakistani–Afghani border that was to be sold in Europe— after being routed through Africa via sea or air.

If Emmanuel was eventually pushed out or had drugs seized and crews arrested, Pauline didn't know, but he refocused his energies in South Asia—mainly Burma and Thailand. So when she started up with him, he was smuggling grade-three and grade-four heroin—what Pauline called "burn" and "pure," respectively. The number-three grade of heroin is the smokable form, while number four, which is purer, is the powder form. Emmanuel's supply was good—Burma was one of the chief heroin producers in the world. But still, he had little to show for his business.

"He had people everywhere. Nigerians—you know, even in the goddamn Mongolian desert you'd have some Nigerians. And wherever there was a Nigerian group, Emmanuel was behind them. I used to tell him that he was everywhere, like McDonald's, and when you are in a business like this, it's not a good thing to be on every corner, to be known, you see? He was losing product, people, and, of course, money. He'd have to take on bigger runs or do other jobs to cover debts to suppliers and producers—everyone. And he lost his identity. This is crucial in this business. You need to know what you do—even if it's smuggling drugs, girls, and cigarettes and even if, while doing that, you are working the transport side, the supply side, or selling right out of your bedroom, you need to be clear about what you do. Simple boundaries. That's how you run a business."

Emmanuel had too many irons in the fire, in Pauline's mind. It was like he wanted to get caught. He trafficked heroin but also ran cocaine out of Nigeria to Europe for the

Colombians. He sold methamphetamines to buyers in Spain, sometimes right out of his restaurant. And in the past, he told Pauline, he hadn't been above trafficking thirty or forty workers from Africa to the coast of Spain every now and then.

More recently, she knew, Emmanuel had sold "hot tapped," or stolen, oil through his company in Nigeria. According to international agencies, like Interpol and the United Nations, Nigerian and other African drug smugglers are supposed to be small, loose transactional groups—meaning that they commit crimes of opportunity, as opposed to, say, the Mexican or Colombian drug cartels, which have top-down hierarchies and long, often violent histories of trafficking. Nigerian traffickers had a reputation for getting in, getting out, and then disappearing until the next time.

While this in-and-out approach might be more typical for low-level workers in the trade, like couriers or body packers, runners, and transporters, worldwide, it is rare for an entire drug or criminal syndicate to be this way. However, this catch-as-catch-can structure is supposed to allow entry into the trafficking game to, as the United Nations Office on Drugs and Crime has said, "anyone" in the global West African diasporic communities. Anyone, that is, who can "source, move, and distribute" drugs.

Pauline, Emmanuel, and others in the drug trade could not have known then that this era, the early 1990s, was a sort of renaissance in the history of drug smuggling. In fact, even when I spoke with Pauline or any of her associates about this period, they did not mark this moment as having been special in any particular way. And because they did not deem it such, perhaps I should not either, but looking at it from the vantage point of 2010, nearly twenty years on and many research, media, and policy reports later, I see just how "advanced" drug traffickers out of Africa were.

Perhaps it was because of a combination of factors: distracting headlines out of Africa—civil wars in Liberia, Sierra Leone, and Somalia; poverty; natural disasters; genocide in Rwanda—and the astonishing misperception that the African continent held little strategic geopolitical or economic importance. Perhaps these events kept African gangs off the radar of law enforcement all over the world and allowed rival global organized-crime groups—the Italians, the Colombians, the Jamaicans, the Albanians—to think of the Nigerians and other African syndicates as less of a threat. It seems as if groups as diverse as Interpol and the Mafia could not fathom the rise of well-funded and well-organized African drug-smuggling rings. But in the mid-1990s, when I first spoke to low-level African drug couriers in Rebibbia, all of them worked for African networks—from Nigerian to Tanzanian.

Despite whatever law-enforcement oversight permitted Emmanuel's business to flourish in the late 1980s and '90s, UN documents and academic research seem to indicate that by the mid- to late 1990s, there was a corrective effort because officials became aware, based on increased seizures of large quantities of drugs, of the growing importance of Africa in the international drug trade.

While aspects of Emmanuel's business fit the profile of what the UN and others deemed "common traits" of West

African traffickers (subcontracted foreign girls who smuggled drugs via planes, varied legal and illegal businesses, and criminal contacts throughout Nigerian immigrant communities globally), Emmanuel was also very different from the stereotypical suspect. Unlike many of the Nigerian smugglers at the time, who shied away from cartel-like structures by keeping their business small—employing only either family members or close friends, and usually never more than three or four people per crew—Emmanuel was a man who sat on top of a budding international business empire, both legal and illegal. He had proven himself and kept his eyes on profit.

Pauline knew this; it was why she felt that she needed to learn from him. And above all, for all his faults, his short temper, and his sloppy business practices, Pauline felt certain about one thing: Once she set him right, she was going to make lots of money with Emmanuel.

CHAPTER 22.

Ourselves or Nothing

MARY REMEMBERED THAT THERE was a certain quality of stillness during the day. The morning sun baked the muddy holes into solid ruts, only to be softened by the rains that came in the afternoon. With no work and nothing to do, the refugees sat under whatever shelter they could find and watched the weather change.

"We were all starving." Mary said. "None of us had the energy to move. And when we did, it was only to accept the charity of a bag of rice or to fight over a cassava."

The nighttime brought out the demons. "All through the night, you could hear the small cries of women. It was a widow's cry. We would muffle our sounds in our hands, in the rags that we brought with us, into the backs of our children.

We may not have spoken to each other when the sun was up, but this is how we spoke at night.

"You don't know what it is like to be a refugee. To live in another person's country, it is hell itself. Liberians were like an illness that the Nigerians didn't want to catch. They worried that we would bring our war with us, that we would spoil their lies about their own country. Nigerians lived without their freedoms, just as we Liberians did under our government, but we were contaminated because we created war, and we were at their mercy.

"After we arrived in Nigeria, we went first to a camp and then later to live in a church for refugees. It was a very difficult time, but I put my trust in God and prayed that one day easier times would fall upon me and my children. There was very little I could do to help myself. The war had locked up my ability to care for myself. I could not go to any embassy, because of my family's connection to the fighting. I changed my name and had no documents, so I was a woman who could not prove who she was. I became like many of the Liberians living in Nigeria—we were like the walking dead. We existed in our own minds, we saw each other, but nobody else seemed to notice us. When they did, they were scared."

FROM 1989 TO 1997, the United Nations reported, there were some 141,000 Liberian refugees living in Nigeria. Mary and her sons left Liberia in the early days of the conflict and went to Oru Camp, in Ogun State, one of the largest refugee camps in western Africa. During much of the first Liberian civil war, Nigeria was controlled by the notoriously corrupt and brutal dictatorships of Ibrahim Babangida and Sani Abacha.

The conditions in the camp were abysmal. The ground was wet and muddy with the rains. Dogs and people seemed to fight for the same places to sleep, the same scraps of food. "We became animals. We were ruined, you understand. Whoever we were before the war, whatever our dreams, they were nothing, meant nothing, when the fighting began, so I guess that is why we were refugees. In Nigeria, it didn't matter—our past or our future, what we had seen or felt, who we had lost. All of us in that camp shared the same common thread: We were Liberian, and we were dirt poor." Soon, Mary left the camp and went to a nearby church that allowed refugees to live on its grounds.

MARY PULLED HER HANDS together as if she were praying. It was her way of stopping herself from going too deeply into her life at the camp and the church. She fell silent, perhaps separating out what was important for her to share from what was too painful. The silence caused the guard at the nearby desk to notice us and ask, "Are you done?"

Without turning in the guard's direction, Mary quickly replied, "No. We'll be needing more time." The guard sighed and went over to the corner by the windows. She stared outside.

The interruption severed Mary from her memories of the camp. Speaking with a stronger voice, she asked, "Did I tell you that I have four school degrees? I was educated in business." I knew Mary had gone to school, and figured that she had even gone to university, but still, I was impressed. "It's true," she said, smiling with pride, "and I am quite a good business lady.

"That's why, when I was in Nigeria, it was so difficult for me. I looked for work, but they can't even feed their own natives, so what could I do?

"I looked good once, you know." Mary stated this as a matter of fact.

I didn't know where she was going with that statement, but having been taught the ways of polite exchange in my American schools, I smiled. Yet Mary mistook my smile as a gesture of disbelief.

Her eyes flashed with indignation, and she said, "Really, I was—I was pretty then."

"No, no, of course you were. I think you're pretty now—that's why I smiled," I stammered, trying to correct the misunderstanding.

"All right, all right. I don't have anger toward you. I just want to explain." Mary waited until I nodded dumbly for her to go on.

"I was really at the last of my ropes, Asale. I couldn't get work. I had no family or friends who could offer assistance. I didn't know what to do, so I took to selling my body. I had children to feed. I'll tell you, it was not an easy choice to get into this line of work. I lost my self-respect and asked for God to forgive my poor woman's choices.

"While in this line of work, I made a friend, Eddie. I guess you could say that he became my boyfriend. He offered me protection and some money. He made my living conditions at the church for refugees bearable. I sent my children to school with his assistance. He helped me a lot when I was conducting this line of business, you know."

"Did he ever take any money from you?" I asked, curious if Eddie had been more like a pimp than like a savior.

"Yes, sometimes he did. And I gave it to him. I know what you are asking, and yes, he did profit off my back, but not always. And besides, he had done so much for me that I was happy to be able to repay him just a little. You see, Eddie was not a common man. People knew who he was. He had some money, you know. Eddie could see how much I was fighting for my life, and he offered to help me start a business. I was going to become a market woman. He told me that he would take me to another country so I could buy clothing that I could sell at the market. Market women can make good earnings, and I liked the idea of being a business lady again. I was very happy.

"We traveled to Singapore together. It was a three-week trip. When we arrived, he gave me $3,000 U.S. I had never seen that much money! It was money, he said, to buy the merchandise that I would sell in the market. I took $1,000 and hid it for the children. With the rest, the $2,000, I knew I could buy what I needed to sell."

"Did you wonder how he got the money for the trip?" I asked.

"No, because you have to understand that he had money all the time; he often traveled." She repeated, "Everyone knew him, Asale. He was not a common man." Mary was sitting on the edge of her seat, trying to make her world big enough that I could fit in it.

CHAPTER 23.
Temporary Assignment

I HAD TURNED INTO a stalker. Despite feeling wounded by Albert, by his shouting and cursing at me, I made it my mission to bring him around. I gave him a week to cool down, which was when I was due to pick up the glasses I'd ordered from the optical shop. I hoped to have another chance to talk to him, but when he saw me coming in the front door that day, he beelined for the storeroom. I decided to wait for him after work. At first I stayed across the street, out in the open, so that he could see me, just in case he had changed his mind and wanted to talk. He didn't.

I came back the next day and the next, but either he had those days off or was using a back door, so I planned a surprise attack. I decided to come a little earlier and wait right by the front door. It would be an ambush but I hoped that I could start pleading my case immediately. But as I walked up to the store, I knew that all was not going to go according to plan.

A guy was sitting on a Vespa parked on the sidewalk, right by the store's door. He was young, about Albert's age, and I suspected they were friends. I hoped that I was wrong. I tried to make myself look busy by pulling out a book and leaning against the wall. There was no place to sit, and the sun, though setting, was still strong enough to beam directly into my eyes. I was squinting. Finally, I had to hold the book up over my head for shade. The boy on the Vespa watched me with amused curiosity. I knew I looked absurd, but I was determined not to leave my spot. If I did, within a matter of minutes, I knew Albert would be gone and I would have to come back and do it all again.

The boy on the bike saw Albert first. *"Che fai, stronzo!"* he said, laughing. Though he had just called Albert a shit, it was clear that they were good friends. Albert bounded over to the Vespa, laughing and playfully telling his friend to fuck off. I walked up to them quickly, nervous that Albert was going to hop on the back of the scooter and disappear. I caught the eye of his friend first. I gave him a smile that I hoped was friendly but also had some gravitas.

"Albert," I said in English, breaking into their banter. I stood an arm's length away from him. I didn't want to get too close. "Can we talk for a minute? I need to apologize to you."

Albert turned and looked at me, more embarrassed than angry that I had dared to speak to him in front of his friend.

His eyes darted around nervously. It looked like he was trying to find a hole in the ground to swallow him. And then I saw it: There was a vulnerability to Albert that I had not paid attention to before. He was a kid who had raised himself, and he had done a good job. But still, he bore the look of someone who had been stripped of his foundation. To me, he seemed to be a boy who had been looking for humanity but who had unwittingly gone searching for it in empty cupboards.

Suddenly, I felt terrible, awful. "I am really very sorry. I . . . I am sorry. I'll leave you alone." I stumbled away from them, shocked at my own stupidity and arrogance. I wanted to walk down the street banging my palm against my forehead and repeating, "What was I thinking?" out loud over and over. Why couldn't I just leave this poor guy alone? He had clearly told me to stay away, but I had decided that I needed him. Worst of all, I had violated a clear request.

When I got home, I called a friend of mine in the States. I needed to confess my bad behavior to a partial judge. "Don't worry about it," she soothed. "You don't even know this guy. Who cares what he thinks?" Well, I did, I told her.

"But why?" And then she paused. "Is this about your research, or is something else going on here?"

She was a historian. The people she was interested in were long dead. She worked safely in the archives, with books, pieces of paper. And, of course, that had its own dangers. Books can captivate you, worm into your mind and make you talk about them obsessively, but you can close them and choose to leave them or take them with you, return to them at your own convenience. Frankly, I was jealous of my historian friend. She could do with books what I wanted to be able to do with my work at Rebibbia: pick it up and set it down when I wanted, treat the prison like a library and neatly file in alphabetical order each person I met there.

Was there something else going on here? Yes, there was. I had made Albert an extension of me. We shared a similar history: Both of our parents had been incarcerated, we were roughly the same age, and somehow, over many months, I had decided that his mother seemed a lot like my father, if only because they were both drug smugglers.

I knew it was wrong, this conflation. But when I was a kid, I didn't meet anyone, aside from my sister, whose parents had been in prison at one point, let alone someone whose parent had also smuggled drugs across international borders. That changed, of course, as I got older, but in 1970, the year, or one of the years, that my father went to prison, only three hundred thousand people were incarcerated in the United States, and only 3 percent of those people were held on drug charges. In relative terms, that was nothing compared with today's prison population of over two million.

So I couldn't help but feel I needed to know Albert. But I didn't tell my friend this—the "something" she was inquiring about would not be the "something" of my response. "No," I answered. "There's nothing going on—no attraction, if that's what you mean. It's about my research. That's all."

"Research is research. You will get whatever information you think you need from him from someone else. And really, who cares what he thinks? Rome is a huge city. It's not like you'll ever see him again, so let it go," she said.

I was going to try.

CHAPTER 24.
Uganda

IT WAS A LONG flight. When they finally touched down in Entebbe, Pauline jumped to her feet in relief. She had been squeezed between Jojo and Emmanuel for thirteen hours, and she couldn't wait to put some distance between her and Jojo. Since they'd left London, where they had caught their connecting flight, Jojo's body had oozed over Pauline's armrest and seat and into their limited legroom space. "As we got closer to Africa, I could feel him sweating on me," she told me. "It was disgusting."

What also disgusted her was the way Emmanuel had slept all the way to Uganda, covering his head and body with three blankets. To Pauline's recollection, he hadn't even moved to use the toilet or to eat or drink. So, instead of having an in-depth conversation with him about the future of their business together, she had listened to Jojo quibble with the flight attendants about giving him extra trays of food, more snacks, and stronger coffee.

But she forgot all about her anger when she stepped off the plane and stood at the top of the stairs. Looking out over the runway and beyond into Entebbe, Pauline was suddenly very glad to be home. It had been years—five, six, seven . . . she could hardly remember the last time she had been in Uganda. The smells of diesel fuel, burning garbage, and cooking spices were all the unmistakable scents of her childhood; the constant music, the playful shouting, the laughter that followed all brought her back to a more familiar side of herself. *I have been in Europe too long,* she thought. But she didn't let nostalgia take over. She didn't have time. When she reached the bottom of the steps, she saw Henry. He smiled at her with his big, generous face, which made her realize she was also smiling back at him.

"Eh-hey, cousin!" Henry said as he half hugged her by giving her a hard pat on the back. He then turned and greeted Emmanuel and Jojo, who seemed to appear from nowhere. Henry's assistant walked them to a SUV parked near the end of the runway. Pauline took charge of the situation, knowing that she needed to set the tone for this trip and her return to Spain. Things had to be different, starting this very moment. She turned to Jojo and, pointing to the assistant, said, "Go with this chap here and get the bags."

Jojo hesitated. Pauline saw him look at Emmanuel for directions, but she didn't stick around to see if her orders would be followed. She just knew that they had better be. They were on her territory now.

On their way to the hotel, it seemed that Henry and Emmanuel had become fast friends, teasing each other about wives and mistresses. Jojo was sitting up front with the driver, sulking. Pauline took the opportunity to look out the window and watch the passing scenery. When they reached Kampala nearly an hour later, she felt as if she and the city were old lovers: The time and distance had left them both changed, but somehow they were still, in fundamental ways, the same.

They made their way to an affluent area in Kampala where Jojo and Emmanuel were staying at a hotel. Pauline would stay at Henry's house in Nakasero, which was virtually down the road from Emmanuel. She wanted to keep a close eye on Henry and make sure that she wasn't squeezed out of any of the conversations that were going to happen on this trip. At her core, Pauline trusted Henry, but she knew that he was not above trying to cut anyone out of a deal if it meant that he could make more money. She couldn't fault him, though—she knew she was the same way.

When they said their goodbyes to Jojo and Emmanuel, Henry chided Pauline for making them stay in a hotel.

"They should be staying with me. My house is better than this hotel. What must they think of our hospitality?"

Pauline wasn't worried about keeping up appearances of a proper Ugandan welcome. Instead she answered, "What would your wife say about you coming home with me and two Nigerians? You think Amina would not have any questions for you? Don't tell me your pride is getting in the way of your clear thinking. If you want to show Emmanuel that you are a big man, have him come over, treat him to some of our local food, take him to your lake house, buy him expensive dinners. I don't really care. But I don't want any billboards. Be discreet."

Henry backed away from the conversation. He wasn't a man who liked to fight openly. He had better ways of dealing with people who made him angry. It was Pauline's turn to backpedal now—she had said too much. She couldn't afford to lose his support, so she apologized. The stress of getting to Uganda and the strange but also wonderful feeling of being home had her on edge. She needed rest and a shower, and then, she told her cousin, "We can talk about all the money we are going to make."

At Henry's house, his wife, Amina, was there, waiting for them. If Amina was surprised to see Pauline after all those years away, she didn't show it. In fact, it was as if no time had passed between them. Amina handled Pauline in the same way in which all the women in Charles's family did: It didn't matter if they had been born into the clan or married in—they all regarded Pauline with disdain tempered with a little bit of fear. As Pauline described it, the women in the family saw her as a "low-class ruffian who bullied her way into the family."

Pauline gave Amina her most gracious smile and said, "Good grief! All these years away, and still the same." Turning to Henry, she said, "Henry, you better take your woman to Europe to get some culture, or she'll never get to be First Lady." Pauline laughed loudly, along with Henry, who was pleased by

Pauline's joke. Her jab at Amina fit Henry's requirements for a proper apology: It was a compliment to him at someone else's expense. All was forgiven.

PAULINE FOLLOWED A HOUSEBOY up to her bedroom. She watched as one of her bags knocked against his legs, causing them to bend involuntarily. "It was the funniest thing," she remembered. "He struggled mightily with those bags, but he would not show it. He had a job to do and he was doing it proudly. He wasn't ashamed of who he was. Seeing that boy like that, I knew the first thing that I was going to do was employ someone like him. Because that boy was like me."

When Pauline closed the door to her room to wash up, she paused and looked out over Nakasero Hill. The trees were lush and green, and she could see parts of buildings and houses peeking out between the leaves. Kampala is supposed to be the most Roman of African cities, in that it is reportedly built on seven hills. Kampala was dubbed the City of Eternal Green, and Rome, the Eternal City, yet neither lived up to its name in Pauline's mind. Kampala was green but dusty, and when there wasn't dust, there was mud. And nothing was timeless about Rome—it was all vestiges of the past. But both places had brought her here, to this moment. Kampala was both the future and the past, but more important, it was home—a place that by nature made Pauline have to work hard. She had to keep up appearances, mind the Ugandan way of doing things. She was less free to be herself here.

Rome, on the other hand, was easy. She hated the city at times, but what she gained in Rome—the perspective and the ability to be fully herself—was, to her, the very definition of freedom.

Pauline had left Uganda promising not to return, and yet she was back. Only this time she wasn't just the "low-class ruffian" wife of an aspiring civil servant. When she was younger, she had gotten behind Charles and pushed him because he was her fastest way to a better, bigger life. He had the better education, the family connections, and the wealth that she did not have. The ways of Kampala, of Uganda, had forced her to be this way, she reckoned.

Suddenly, staring out the window in the unfamiliar room, she felt very alone. It was a brief and fleeting moment, but she wished she could be back in Rome and put this trip behind her. "Maybe," she wondered long after the fact, "maybe it was being home after all that time, maybe it was the months of hardships and fights with Emmanuel to get us to this place, maybe I just wanted to already be where I wanted to go. . . . I wanted to have the future already behind me."

CHAPTER 25.
Singapore

MARY'S BOYFRIEND, "EDDIE," HAD been to Singapore before. After they landed, she went right to work, buying items that she would sell. For the first time since the massacre of her family, Mary had a feeling that she had not experienced: dignity. "Going out and buying what I needed for my own business . . . oh, I felt that I woke up from being dead. I was making my way back to being who I was before the war. It was freedom."

It must have been, because I had never seen Mary look so radiant as she told me about walking the strange streets of Singapore, eating foods that she'd never known about, bartering with shopkeepers for the best prices, hiring taxis to take her back to her hotel because she had managed to buy so much. Within a few days, she was making her way around the city on her own, coming back in the evening exhausted but burning with determination to get her life back on her terms.

One evening after ten days of being in Singapore, she returned to the hotel room and waited for Eddie to show up. The last few days, he had been telling her that he had business that he had to attend to, and that was why he was arriving at the hotel late or leaving very early in the morning. It didn't matter to her. She liked having time for herself.

THE NEXT MORNING, HE still wasn't back. Mary was worried but decided that she would be patient and carry on with her business. A full week after he had disappeared, the phone rang in the middle of the night, waking her up. It was Eddie. He apologized over and over again, telling her that he had had to travel to Japan for business unexpectedly, and that he had wanted to call her beforehand but hadn't been able to.

"Here I had sat for a week, fussing and worrying about this man, not sure if he was dead or alive, not sure if I should stay in Singapore or if I should leave. It was a hard time. But when I heard him on the phone and he was telling me that he had business in Japan, I just knew . . . I knew that he was lying to me." Mary was shaking her head slowly, working her way back through her memory, as if imploring the self that was in Singapore to act differently, to get out while she could, to be less trusting.

"He said he would be back the next day, so I waited for him. Two days passed, and still he didn't show. Well, all of this was upsetting my system, and when I got my menses, I had, as I always do, terrible cramps. But this time it was even more painful. Oh, Asale, I was in so much pain, I took to the bed for three days, thinking that I was dying.

"Now, here is part of my story that I can hardly believe myself, but I assure you this is what happened, as God is my witness. I was in that bed, not thinking about anything but my pain, and my boyfriend, he came back. He found me in the bed and was comforting to me. He told me that I was to fly out the next day to go back to Nigeria. There was a side of me that didn't want to go, as I was feeling ill and wasn't sure about the journey. But then I wanted to be back with my children; I was thinking about getting out of the hotel, starting up that life that I wanted. So I agreed.

"This was when he deceived me, while I was in bed. He offered to help me ready my things, saying that he wanted me to be rested. I had many pieces of luggage, mostly filled with all of the things I hoped to sell in the market."

As he packed up her bags, Mary's boyfriend broke the news that he wouldn't be flying back to Nigeria with her. He told her that he had to stay in Singapore a few more days to finish up his business. She didn't question him. He had been gone so long that her first thought was not that he had business, but that he had another woman in Singapore whom he was seeing. She didn't care anymore.

When Mary was half-asleep, he woke her to give her instructions about her arrival in Lagos. Nothing unusual, she remembered, just that he had bought some gifts for his brother that he wanted her to carry back with her.

"But I have never met your brother. How can I give him your gifts?" she asked him.

He told her not to worry, that the brother knew where Mary lived and that he would come by to collect his packages.

"By the good grace of God, I swear I never troubled over that moment until much later. He had given me money to start my business. I was thinking about that and my children. I just wanted to get back to them. You know, I felt like I had been gone a long time."

The next morning, still feeling sick but eager to get back to Nigeria, Mary boarded an Alitalia flight from Singapore to Rome, where she would meet a connecting flight to Lagos. She had never been to Europe before—in fact, she had never traveled outside Africa—so she was excited when she landed in Rome. Even though she was going to be sitting at the airport for only a few hours, it made her feel as though she could add another country to the list of places she had been.

While she stood in line at the passport control, Mary was feeling good—strong, even. "When I was on that plane from Singapore to Roma, I made so many plans. I was passionate about achieving success and convinced that I was going to get on top of my new life in Nigeria."

FOREIGN PASSENGERS MOVED THROUGH the queue slowly, readying their passports and papers, preparing to move quickly when they were called to the booth. The line was long, almost out the door. It was July and very hot in Rome.

The opening and closing of the door between the tarmac and the inside of the airport dissipated the blast of cold air from the air-conditioning, leveling the temperature to a manageable lukewarm. A few families ahead of her, Mary saw two men dressed in blue uniforms move through the line. She didn't pay attention to them until they approached her.

"They spoke in very broken English, but I understood what they were saying. They said the words *passaporto* and *tickets*. I had everything in a pocket, right here." She patted her left breast. "They asked me where I was coming from, and I told them." The two men went on to the person behind her.

Mary waited patiently for her turn at the booth. The young man hardly looked at her as he collected her documents, stamped her passport briskly, and called for the next person in line.

The airport in Rome, Fiumicino, felt smaller than the one in Singapore. It was also not as nice, it seemed to Mary as she looked around the airport on the way to the gate for the flight to Lagos. *So this is Europe?* Mary thought to herself. She found her gate and sat watching her fellow travelers. She decided that she was not impressed.

She didn't have long before her next flight, about an hour, and she was starting to turn her mind back to Lagos. The first thing that she wanted to do was get out of the church for refugees. She wanted to have her own home again, focus on creating a stable life for the children. The church was fine and truly a godsend, but it wasn't good, she thought, for the children to be living with refugees. Liberia was her home, always would be, but she knew that she could not go back there, not anytime soon and maybe not ever. She had to put down roots in Nigeria. She had to start the moment she returned, she vowed.

As she sat and stared and let her mind wander back and forth between Lagos, the airport, and her time in Singapore, a man in a uniform approached her.

"He spoke English, but he didn't say anything more to me. He just asked for my passport. I gave it to him. He looked at it and handed it back to me. I was confused but not troubled. I was the only person he spoke to; there were so many people around me, watching what was happening."

She sat for a while, trying to put the incident out of her mind. Mary willed her thoughts to drift back to her plans for a new life in Nigeria, but she couldn't focus. When the flight attendant started calling passengers for the flight, she didn't know why, but she felt some relief. Like everyone in the waiting area, she started to gather up her bags and was about to make her way toward the line forming near the runway door.

She couldn't recall clearly what happened next. One minute she was bending down, picking her bag up off the floor; the next she was surrounded by fifteen police officers.

"They started shouting at me in Italian. I had no idea what they were saying. There was an Italian man who was traveling to Lagos who had been sitting next to me, and he started translating for me."

The Italian man told Mary that the officers wanted her to go with them. She froze. They were calling her flight; if she left with them, she wouldn't get on the plane. She looked at the translator. He was sitting calmly in his chair, newspaper in hand. There didn't seem to be any urgency.

"I have to get on the plane. I'm going home," Mary told him.

"Without saying anything to the police standing around me, he said that they had some questions for me and that I needed to go with them. That is when I started to get agitated. A guard put his hand on me, trying to pull me toward them. I remember shouting, 'Wait!' or something like that. I didn't know what this was all about. I wasn't sure how long they wanted to speak to me, I wasn't sure if they would hold the plane. I knew nothing."

One of the officers picked up her hand luggage, and the others closed in around her. Mary's head was spinning in a sea of blue uniforms. In a haze, she realized that their sheer force in numbers was leading her away from the waiting area, away from the plane that would take her to her children.

"They took me into a small room, and there on the floor I could see that all of my bags had been opened—my clothes, the merchandise I had been about to sell in the market . . . everything was laying out on the floor and on a table. They, the police, started shouting at me in Italian. I didn't understand, until I caught a word that they kept shouting over and over again: '*droga, droga.*' It was clear then that they thought I had drugs, and I knew that I didn't.

"I started getting violent then. I was shouting at them in English, they were shouting at me in Italian. It was chaos. I couldn't make them understand me. I kept saying, 'Wait, wait.' It was all moving too fast for me.

"They started pulling out packages from my bags, cutting them open. Oh! There were so many of them. They showed me what was inside. That is when I fainted. I had never seen drugs before, but I knew that what they showed me were drugs. I was deceived. It was as if in that moment, all the lies that I could not see before were made as clear as water."

A little while later, as Mary sat in the small room, waiting to see what her fate would be, a police translator finally arrived to speak to her. She told him everything. She gave him the name of her boyfriend, the name and street address of the hotel. She answered all of his questions. But even then, she knew that it didn't matter. The police would not go after a man who was thousands of miles away. No, the police had her and that was good enough.

"I knew that I was going to go to prison and that there was nothing that I could do. I tried very quickly to resign myself to God's will. Oh, but I cried thinking about my children. They'd think that I'd abandoned them. Even before I went to court and heard my fate of six years' imprisonment, I knew that they would think that I had left them to fend on their own.

"You know," Mary said ponderously, "I am not bitter. Yes, this man lied to me and used my vulnerable situation to profit himself. But I am angry with myself. I am angry that I could not see the trap I walked into, angry that I was greedy for a life without the memories of my country, my husband. Mostly I am angry because I was stupid.

"Every night as I go to bed, I hear the last words that I remember the Italian man at the airport saying to me. He said, 'In Italy they don't joke.'"

CHAPTER 26.
I Belong Here

PAULINE WAS DISAPPOINTED IN the outcome of the Ugandan trip. By the time she and Emmanuel made it back to Spain, they had reached an agreement that would allow her to buy out a small portion of his heroin trade, which she would move from Spain to Italy. In practical terms, it looked something like this: Emmanuel would earn 15 percent off her business, simply by franchising his operation. This was different from his "pre-Pauline" arrangement, in which he had a handful of crews, usually small groups of men who acted as contract employees. Those crews were responsible for outsourcing different jobs to get the drugs and then move, process, and distribute them.

Pauline's job was supply and shipping or, as she called it, "import-export." Emmanuel earned a profit from Pauline's import-export by sharing his supply sources without doing any additional work. Cousin Henry loaned her a sum of money that she had to pay back with 20 percent interest. (Though Pauline did not disclose the exact amount to me, I estimated it to be upwards of $250,000, given the amount of drugs she said she purchased.) Her agreement with Henry also brought with it some secured lines of transporting heroin from Asia to a port in Kenya, a commercial airstrip in Uganda, and money-laundering opportunities in the growing Ugandan economy. But there was a downside, too.

"I was being swindled," Pauline recalled. "I was so eager to get my own piece of land in this trade that I agreed to terms that would make any smart woman take a machete to her opponent!" Only Pauline didn't know whom to fight first—Emmanuel's terms were mostly fair for the first few runs, but she didn't want to work for him permanently. And Henry's conditions—the interest rate on his loan, on top of his demand for an additional 10 percent of her profits—was too much. She managed to get him down to 7 percent. "I was robbed blind before I could even start. Nearly half of my profit, and my chance to increase my profit and eventually expand and earn more money, had been bartered away to these assholes."

Pauline knew that she needed to get out of these deals as fast as she could. "It's not like I wanted to be a drug dealer for the rest of my life," she told me. "Trust me, a whore has a better chance at growing old in her profession than a drug dealer."

Still, there was little she could do at the moment. She put all her plans of getting out from under these guys aside until she could build up a crew in Italy and establish herself.

Pauline's Italian business would be, by necessity, a little different from Emmanuel's: She was going to focus on procuring drugs and shipping them from their place of origin to their destination. She preferred to deal in large quantities and wanted to stay away from processing, or "cutting," drugs. "The problem was," she said once, "that I was limited in Italy. The Italians and the Albanians controlled a lot of the market. If I wanted to stay small, run some pills and some powder to the discos up and down the coast, fine. But I would have to sell to a thousand kids a night to even come close to making the money I wanted to make. And distribution? Forget it! There is no going up against the Italians on their own soil. That's just not done. So I had to offer a service—I had to offer better than the Chinese, the East Europe dudes, the Moroccans."

With over 40 percent of her earnings going to Henry and Emmanuel, Pauline's idea of filling a niche did not seem promising. In her mind, the only way to earn a significant amount of money was to control as much of the drug business, from growing to selling, as possible. Everyone knew that in the international drug trade, where raw heroin might come from central or Southeast Asia, with the ultimate destination being Europe or the United States, many borders needed to be crossed, people needed to be paid on both sides of those borders, drugs needed to be cut, cooked, and repackaged at secure locations, and the people who did that work also needed to be paid, as did the people or companies that owned the factories that processed the drugs.

Then those repackaged drugs had to be transported again—trucks, boats, and planes rented or bought, or airline, train, or bus tickets purchased. Couriers paid, drivers paid, pilots paid, ground crew paid, customs officials paid. All of this had to be done before drugs could hit the streets to be sold and profits could be made. Pauline knew all of this, yet she was not deterred. When she had worked for the Italians and, later, even with Emmanuel, she had seen what success looked like, had been up close to realizing a life that she wanted for herself. She wasn't going to back away from that, even if it meant paying 40 percent.

CHAPTER 27.

Straight Is the Gate,
Narrow Is the Way

ONE AFTERNOON, PAULINE NUDGED me a bit closer
to her world. "Stop hiding out in this prison. I want you to
take your notebook out there," she said, pointing toward a
window. "There is nothing this room can teach you about me.
You want to know more, go out there."

"What do you mean?" I asked, though I didn't have to. I
had already met at least three people in prison who worked for
Pauline directly, as well as a handful of other, lower-level operatives who said they didn't know whom they actually worked
for but assumed it was the infamous Ugandan. Pauline had
suggested before that she might be open to letting me meet
with some of her people who were still working the trade to,

as she put it, "get her story right." But this was the first time
she had actually given me a directive. I of course didn't mention my attempts to contact Albert, and I couldn't help but be
curious about the people on the outside she might put me in
touch with.

"Look, you have been coming to see me for a while.
That's a good thing. But I am going to introduce you to some
people. I want you to meet them. They will help you with your
research."

I looked at Pauline. This was the first time she had even
mentioned my research. I had seen her almost every week,
sometimes twice a week, for nearly a year now, and the one
thing that bothered me most about our exchanges was that
she treated all of our interviews as if my sole purpose were to
record her life story. She had turned me into her official biog-
rapher. She gave me little pieces of papers with the names of
girls she had gone to school with back in Uganda. She wrote
out a list of her favorite foods, colors, music, and movies. She
made recommendations of books I should read, mostly famous
biographies or autobiographies of historical figures: Albert
Einstein, Kwame Nkrumah, and Winston Churchill.

I never knew if she was conflating her life with these
men's, but that was what I liked about Pauline: You could
never be sure whether she was all bluster or had a strong love
of irony. So, just as she never acknowledged my research or the
fact that I was not coming to Rebibbia purely to meet with
her, there was something about her air of self-importance that
never seemed like full-blown arrogance. Pauline was the center

of her own universe, and she was very generous in allowing other people to make her the focus of their world, too.

For a while, I was all too happy to visit with her and listen to her stories, which she usually recounted with much bravado, and then go on about the rest of my day speaking to other detained women. But increasingly, I was seeing less and less of those other women. The prison administrators seemed to be growing tired of my visits; I was an unnecessary intrusion on the prison's daily function, and because of that, I was having a harder time gaining access to the place. Before, I could call up a day or two in advance and let Maria or one of the other administrators know that I wanted to come and do some interviews. Increasingly, I was kept waiting on the phone or told to call back only to have it ring and ring, until I finally hung up. Other days I would show up at my prearranged meeting time only to be sent back home.

And then when I *was* allowed into Rebibbia, some women who used to talk to me stopped showing up for interviews. I wasn't sure why there was this sudden change, but the only constant was Pauline. I never seemed to have any problems getting in to see her. So, of course, when I started seeing Pauline twice a week for a while and no one else, I couldn't help but feel that she had set it up this way.

So when she urged me to meet with her crew, I was nervous but also grateful to get out from underneath her presence in the prison, because even before knowing Pauline, I had developed a morbid fascination with drug smuggling that I tried to keep hidden from everyone, including and especially her. I wanted insight into her world, despite knowing the dangers it posed, in part because it was as close to my father as I was ever going to get. And because I was uncomfortable about this fact, meeting her crew was not incentive enough for me to agree to it. Actually, there was another, more pragmatic reason why I didn't flat-out refuse the offer. Because I spent most of my days either in the library or at Rebibbia, I had few friends in Rome. My very good friend Stefano was away in Paris, doing his own research, and my friends from Naples hardly ever traveled up to see me, nor did I go to see them. The weight of my days in Rebibbia was becoming a burden. I had become a vessel of stories of some of the worst things that could happen to women: rape, abuse, wartime torture, witnessing the deaths of loved ones, losing their children, their sisters, their husbands. These were women who had been sold and bought and sold again, and some, in desperation, had sold themselves or killed in order to gain a different kind of freedom in prison.

Yet going to Rebibbia structured my days. It gave me purpose, meaning. Without my interviews, I feared I would become just another tourist. I contemplated returning to the male prison, as I had done in the early days of my research, but my memories of some of the men I had met there, the ones who were responsible for raping and beating and sell-ing women—some of the very women whom I had come to know from the women's prison—sickened me so much that I decided to stop my work in the men's ward. I decided I wasn't that desperate, at least not yet.

As much as I hated to admit it, I needed a break from prison. I had grown weary of trying to keep up appearances. Every time I left Rebibbia, I left bigger and bigger chunks of myself inside. Month after month of painful stories and mournful regrets about the seemingly small and ill-thought-out decisions that had shattered the lives of so many women had led me into the unfamiliar terrain of depression. I felt myself teetering on the brink of an unbearable sadness, and I knew that I needed to reach out to the world and stop "living" in prison if I was going to try to stay in Italy for much longer.

I had attempted to call my loved ones back in the States, but I had soon realized that I couldn't convey with precise words what was troubling me. My inarticulateness caused my family to worry. My twin sister, perhaps working off instinct, pleaded with me to come home. But I couldn't. I felt as if I would be abandoning people, women who had relied on me to listen and to talk and to respond to their letters. Many of these women were my friends, and we each needed each other for different reasons. I needed to stay as much as I needed a break. So when Pauline extended an invitation to me to get a glimpse of what her life on the outside had been like, it appeared as a window left open for me to climb through.

All of this ran through my mind when I accepted Pauline's offer. I was ready, and even cautiously excited when I met Hassan, Jojo, and Luca at Wimpy's. I knew that leaving the safe confines of prison to hang out with active criminals was reckless and potentially really stupid. But I felt safe. I kept telling myself that I had the cover of academic research and I was not required to, nor did I have any intention to, get my hands dirty. I wanted to believe I had control, as if meeting three drug smugglers who moonlighted as an ordinary thug, a human trafficker, and an assassin in a fast food chain was all part of a typical day's work.

CHAPTER 28.
Tomorrow the Past Will Come

IT SHOULD HAVE BEEN quiet. Mary lay awake without anything but a sheet to protect her from the cold. She wore every layer of clothing she had, and had borrowed a pair of socks from one of her cellmates. The women around her, the other women from faraway places, tried to convince her it wasn't cold. "It's summer," they had all told her today, "not cold at all."

"You wait and see," another had said. "When it is winter, you will really know what cold is."

Wait and see—Mary was not sure how long she was going to be in Rebibbia, but she hoped and prayed that she would not have to be there long enough to see winter. Summer or not, she was cold and getting sick from listening to the sound of collective breathing. In a way, it was like being back in Liberia, where she and the children had slept on the floors of other people's homes, or in a school or a football stadium, or among the many others who were so disoriented from the war that they finally stopped trying to go home and just slept in the fields. Gone was any sense that sleep was a private act; now it was just an intimate moment when one's vulnerability was unveiled and put on open display. As she lay listening to the walls breathe and snore and squirm to find a comfortable position, Mary realized that in this sense, prison was more familiar to her than she had ever thought possible.

AFTER THEIR INTERROGATION, THE police had brought her straight from the airport to Rebibbia. She remembered looking out the window of the police car, but instead of seeing the street signs, the buildings, the advances of modern architecture, or glimpses of the material abundance of Europe, she saw only a world map and the countries that lay between her and her children. She thought about the airplane—her airplane—the one that had landed in Nigeria hours ago.

Only about six hours before, she had been getting ready to board a flight. What had happened in the hours since would take her several days to fully comprehend. "Really," Mary said to me, "I thought they had made some very grave error, and that someone would approach me with their apologies and my onward ticket to Lagos."

Mary was not aware that she had arrived at the prison until the car stopped and one of the officers, who only spoke

Italian, told her to get out of the car, or so she gathered from his hand gestures. As three guards led her to Rebibbia's matriculation center, she had no way of knowing that she would not be on the outside of the prison again for another six years.

ON MARY'S FIRST SLEEPLESS night in Rebibbia, she reflected on her life and started to pray, when she realized that the very God she was calling upon for help seemed to have abandoned her long ago. Mary fought back the urge to wail out in grief over everything that God had taken away from her. She reached her hands out to the vacant space beside her, the space that had, save for the last three weeks, always been filled with her sons and before them, her daughter and before her, her husband. For the first time, Mary understood what it was like to die—to go away to an unfamiliar place, to be completely alone with no future in front of her, and to have only memories to keep her company. She felt as if her sternum had been split open.

"When would I ever get to hold the round heads of my sons in my hands and feel their tiny hands on my face when they kissed me?" She held up her hands for me to see. "These two hands, they were for my children. Now who will be there to hold them and to protect them?" Every night for the next six years, this thought would plague her.

CHAPTER 29.
The Oracle

SOMETHING HAPPENED WHEN PAULINE finally returned to Rome. By the time she showed her face one day in the city, late in July, the Roman streets were nearly empty; the Italians had slowly trickled out of the hot city to places either north or south for summer holiday.

When she approached the street where her former apartment was, Pauline saw them, the children and Charles, walking along, chatting excitedly about something they had done that afternoon—the cinema, she guessed. They were too far away to see her, and she was glad for that. She didn't expect them to be outside. In fact, she didn't expect to see them as anything different from what they'd been when she'd left: silent little children who kept their heads down and their faces turned far away from her reach.

She didn't know it until then, when she saw how much her children had grown, but Pauline, who had traveled to Spain, Uganda, Kenya, Nigeria, and England, and even taken a trip to Asia and back through Africa and Europe, had been away from her family for over two years. Her daughter, Isabel, was no longer a toddler, and Albert seemed like a man. Pauline wanted to shout out to them, but Hassan, her right-hand man—her "lieutenant," as she liked to call him, mimicking and mocking Mafiosi hierarchy—was standing next to her. He lit a cigarette and casually said, "Are those the children? They've gotten big!"

"Ah, yes, my ungrateful children. The three of them," she replied snidely.

Pauline watched them walk into the building and decided to come back later on her own. But it would take her another eight months to return to the apartment; by then, her operation would be up and running full bore. During that time, she told herself that she missed the children, but perhaps the real reason she went back for them was to show them what she could provide for them.

She wasted no time moving them out of the apartment and taking Charles with her—not because she loved him, but because it was her duty as a wife. She was still married, a fact that she honored, but the children were not happy with their new apartment, even though it was larger than the old one and they didn't all have to share a room. "The only home they had come to know was that bloody flat I had pulled them from. It was the equivalent of a shack! You couldn't get much lower than that place in all of Rome. They were impossible!" So Pauline didn't concern herself with Charles's or the children's feelings. Later Albert would share with me how they accepted his mother's homecoming with a quiet resentment that made it difficult to be in the same room with her.

Pauline may have had a very unique way—which is to say that she had *no* way, perhaps—of showing her family that she loved them, but she did need them. They helped her feel like she was part of something bigger than her own ambition. She once told me, "I was never blind. I knew that my children and husband hated me. Just as long as they, the children, took my dreams and carried them further than I could, that was all I wanted from them."

But Pauline didn't dwell too long on her family, because business was going well. She had hired herself a good crew—people with whom she had worked in the past, including Hassan. At first, they ran her supply from Spain, but increasingly, their job was hiring other people to do that task. On a trip to Nigeria, separate from Emmanuel, Pauline had met with a Nigerian who ran cocaine for the Colombians. She had signed on to take his supply, offering him cash when the Colombians paid him in coke. And soon she installed two Nigerian brothers, Patrick and Mathew—men I would later meet in prison—to manage this trade for her. The goal for Pauline was to put as much distance between her and the product.

"I was working this business full-time at this stage," she said. "You have to be smart if you are going at this like a hammer—steady, firm, careful. I had already been arrested once when I worked with Bresnik. It was a short stay—they didn't have any evidence—but I did not enjoy losing my freedom. I waited nine months in a cell just to be told that I could go home."

Pauline was making enough money from her cocaine traffic that she thought it was time to renegotiate her deal with Emmanuel and Henry. Doors were opening up for her, and she was preparing to start running her own supply of heroin through Thailand. All she needed to do to set that up was to send Hassan out to meet with suppliers.

Hassan, a handsome Sudanese man and former philosophy-doctorate candidate, had worked various angles of organized crime. Pauline had known him for many years. Hassan balanced Pauline. He had a cooler head, thought things out more carefully, and, importantly, knew when to pull back and walk away from a situation. Pauline also knew that Hassan, despite his lighter touch and his book learning, had seen and done things in his life that she had so far been spared. In Sudan he had been a student activist—imprisoned, tortured, hardened, and sent back out into a world that, in his opinion, showed little justice or mercy. The road that he had taken from there had eventually led him to this moment with Pauline— their shared path, the crimes they had committed and would commit in the future. She would never judge him, not for the things that he had done or for becoming her lieutenant. And he would never judge her for any of her failings, as a mother, a wife, a sister, or a businesswoman. She trusted him. He was closer than a brother. He was her only reliable friend.

So when Hassan told her to jump ship on the Emmanuel deal, Pauline listened and she heard, but she didn't act. She had put some emotional distance between her heart and Emmanuel's sexual indifference toward her, but not entirely. After two shipments had made it to Spain without a problem but could not be delivered to Pauline's people, Hassan had found an alternate supply. "Get out, Pauline," he warned her. "I don't like the smell of this. Rotten. Emmanuel is going to take you down if you hold on too tight. I give you this as a guarantee," he said.

"He was the damned oracle of Delphi, Hassan." Pauline was laughing at the memory, still in awe of Hassan's foresight. "He had seen the future and called in our guy in Spain. Told him to take a holiday. And then he set about saving us from ruin."

Hassan left for Thailand with Pauline's reluctant blessing, and within a month, Emmanuel's apartments in Barcelona had been raided and Jojo and other members of his crew had been arrested. Emmanuel went underground. The first call that he made came through on Pauline's mobile.

"When I heard from him, I was relieved. Really, I think I might have even thanked God." But when Pauline met up with Emmanuel six weeks later at a hotel in Tangiers, Morocco, what she saw made her want to kill him.

CHAPTER 30.
Marooned

AFTER MY INITIAL MEETING at Wimpy's with Hassan, Jojo, and Luca, they developed a habit of showing up
unannounced whenever they wanted. Often, Hassan and
Jojo would be waiting for me in a car at the bus stop near
my house. A couple of times they walked into the grocery
store where I did my shopping, and once they showed up at
my apartment.

Even after I had learned from my first conversation with
Pauline that she had had me followed, I had still given her my
address so that she could write me letters, which she did on
occasion—but I also knew that she would use the information
for more than casual correspondence. So the first time I saw
Hassan and Jojo waiting for me at my local the bus stop, I was
not surprised, though I insisted that we meet at more neutral

locations. But before I knew it, it was getting difficult to keep up with the frequency of our meetings. They took their task seriously and brought me into the fold quickly. I figured it would be only a matter of time before they started dropping by my house. Even so, when the two of them first appeared at my door, I was filled with panic.

It was close to 11:00 AM, and I had spent the morning going over notes from an interview that I had completed a few days before. The buzzer in the foyer sounded with two angry shrieks, but when I asked who was there, I could hear only the *clang* of the gate from the lift. Moments later, there was some shuffling outside the apartment and I opened the door to Hassan and Jojo.

"You can't come in," I told them. "I will meet you outside." When I closed the door on them, I was disoriented. It was strange—I was a little terrified and yet giddy with excitement. I knew that Hassan and Jojo had not come over simply to talk; they wanted to show me something, and I was curious to see it. Without giving it much thought, I grabbed my house keys, my notebook, and my purse and went outside.

Hassan greeted me with a kind smile. I smiled back, happy, in fact, to see him. He always dressed with some care: a brown suede jacket, dark blue jeans, a white shirt, and today a plaid Burberry scarf. It was the casual uniform of most stylish men over forty in Italy. He looked as if he could have been anything: a doctor, a scholar, an architect, or maybe, to a very discerning eye, a drug smuggler, but a benevolent one.

"How did you sleep, Firefly?" Hassan asked as he started walking away from my building down the street toward the bus stop. I followed him.

"Fine, thanks. Where are we off to?"

"Coffee and errands," he said. "What else would we do on a Thursday?"

Frankly, I wouldn't know, I wanted to say. But as we turned the corner and I saw Jojo leaning against the parked car, I started to think that maybe I didn't want to find out.

Based on earlier conversations, I had decided that there was something about Jojo I didn't trust, and knowing that he was a member of Pauline's crew, despite their earlier tension, did not change my opinion. In fact, after I started spending time with Hassan and Jojo, I knew that I didn't like him at all. I had once seen him in the aftermath of a beating he had given someone—I wasn't sure, but I thought it might have been a woman, since less than an hour later, he was on his cell phone, shouting threats and curse words, while a woman cried loudly on the other end of the phone.

With the car in the background and in his yellow T-shirt, tan linen suit, and sunglasses, Jojo looked as if he had jumped out of the set of the 1980s television show *Miami Vice.* It was the end of January, a bit chilly and cloudy. He was obviously trying too hard.

Without speaking, we all climbed into the car and wove our way through the streets of Rome. I had never been in a car with them before; usually we only met in a café or one or two of the restaurants they frequented. I was waiting for trepidation to come over me, but, to my surprise, it didn't. Instead of passively sitting there with a feeling of dread, I reasoned with myself: There was no use in being worried or scared. I had knowingly gotten into the car with these guys, and I knew who they were, what they did for a living. I felt certain that I was not going to willingly participate in anything that was against the law. But if I saw something illegal or violent—what would I do then? I stared out the window at the streets of Rome, as if I could find the answer among the traffic and the pedestrians. This was not a common ethical dilemma for an anthropologist.

"Hey, Hassan," I said, loudly enough that he could hear me from his seat up front, "I'm a researcher, as you know."

"Yes, I know."

"Okay. So, I really don't want to see something that will compromise me." This was too vague, but how else could I politely suggest, *I don't want to go to prison, so don't make me an accomplice?* I added, "I don't want to compromise my research, either. No conflict of interest, right?" I asked, trying to sound lighthearted.

"No conflict of interest. Right," he parroted back.

I nodded my head, believing firmly that we had covered the issue for now.

We pulled up to a block of Soviet era–looking apartments. We had driven for a while, but I knew we were still in Rome. Jojo and Hassan got out. I wasn't sure if they wanted me to go with them or if I should stay behind, so I prepared to wait in the car. The men took a few steps away from the car, and then Jojo turned and opened the door.

He frowned and moved the seat forward. "Come on."

I didn't hesitate. I quickly grabbed my purse and notebook. In my mind, my notebook would let people know that I was not like Hassan and Jojo—that I was not a criminal.

Out on the street, I could hear the faint sounds of children playing. Jojo, Hassan, and I walked toward the building, and I could feel the eyes of two pensioners who stood near the entrance like aged guards. They stared at us, openly and unafraid, as we passed. I didn't dare look at them. I looked at my notebook instead, realizing that nothing could camouflage the strange trio that I formed with Hassan and Jojo. We clearly did not live in the building, and none of us looked like we could even remotely be related to each other. And Hassan and Jojo walked with too much determination to be paying a friendly visit. And then there was me—a young woman who looked even younger than she was and who had a knack for broadcasting her innermost thoughts out loud, on stereo, through her body language alone.

So, given that I felt we were up to no good, I became paranoid that we looked like we were up to no good. I wasn't sure what I was walking into, but I hoped the pensioners would keep whatever suspicions they had to themselves and not call the police.

When we got up to the apartment, I was surprised that it was nearly empty. There were two chairs in the main room; both were filled by men who looked to be in their twenties. I guessed they were from Morocco, but I couldn't be sure.

Hassan got down to business with the men. Though they were speaking in French, I understood that they were discussing money. Hassan motioned for Jojo to go into the other room, and by extension I knew that I had to go with him. Jojo made his way into the kitchen. Reluctantly, I followed.

I was surprised to find a young Italian woman standing at the sink, reading a book and smoking a cigarette. When she saw us, she put her book down and said, "Who's that?" She motioned with her chin in my direction. I hadn't gone to a lot of "business" meetings with Jojo and Hassan, but I had been to enough to know that this was the first time someone had actually noticed me long enough to question why I was there. I found it strange that in a world where it was in people's best interest to be anonymous, it always felt like there were so many people hanging around.

Simona had short blond hair and wore a Che Guevara T-shirt and a thick leather bracelet. She reminded me of some of my friends who studied at the university. I had met other women who worked for Pauline, some of whom were in prison, but Simona was the first Italian woman I had met who either was or passed herself off as a middle-class college student.

After Jojo, Simona, and I had made small talk for more than an hour about music and the places we had traveled to, Hassan walked into the kitchen and gave Simona *bises,* short kisses on each check, a customary greeting that I knew he had picked up from living in Paris. The two of them spoke in French for a few moments before moving into Italian. I let myself slip into the rhythmic cadence of the language. I liked hearing Italian, and Hassan was fluent. If I hadn't known that they were talking about one of the Moroccan men going with

Simona to drop off a parcel to someone named Angelo, I would have found the whole exchange charming and cosmopolitan. Remarkably, I'd already been hanging around Jojo and Hassan for six weeks, and this was the first time I understood that they were talking about drugs. I stood up, wanting to get away from their conversation, and went looking for the restroom.

The bathroom was small, cramped, and dirty; I decided that it was too disgusting to hide out in. I needed to find someplace neutral—if there was such a place. There were some things I just did not want to know. I went looking around the apartment and bumped into one of the Moroccan men I had seen earlier. He was carrying a heavy black bag from the bedroom. I moved out of his way without saying anything. I had reached a dead end and could only turn around and go back to the bathroom or go into the room that he had just come out of.

I quickly glanced inside. The room was empty. I noticed a small balcony off the room and went outside, closing the door behind me. This was as far away as I could get from whatever activity was going on inside the flat. I stood looking over the skyline, dotted with other buildings off in the distance. I had the sudden realization that no one I loved in the world knew where I was at this moment. And if something were to happen to me—say, if the police came busting in and hauled us all away—none of my family members or friends would understand how it was that I had come to be in a room of drug traffickers. I couldn't tell them, for the very reason why I was standing out on the balcony: because it was stupid and ill advised. There were bad people in the world. I didn't like to think about it, but I knew that Jojo and Hassan and maybe Simona and the anonymous Moroccan guy had all personally done things that would give me nightmares. And short of that, they were actively engaged in a deplorable business.

Drugs at almost every level enslaved people—the peasants in Burma or Colombia who were forced to harvest them, the factory workers who earned pennies to process them, the dealers who sold them on the streets, the addicts who ruined their lives over them. My father was one of these people, and my mother too, in her own way, as well as other members of my family who had their own struggles with drugs. And then there was Mary, and the many other women whom I had met in Rebibbia.

Remembering all of these people forced me to ask the questions that I should have asked myself more than a month before: *Why am I doing this? Exactly why am I in this apartment with these people? When did I lose my moral compass?* I had to stop hanging around Jojo and Hassan, I told myself. I had to try to find my way out of this.

But before I could work myself into more of a frenzy, Hassan gently knocked on the balcony door. "Ready to go?"

I stepped through the door. Hassan shook his head once and with real remorse said, "Sorry about that."

I didn't know how to respond.

"Let's eat. I'm hungry." He quickly changed the subject. "There's a really good Turkish restaurant. It's on the way to your place. I'll drop you after."

"I don't know," I said.

"Oh, come on. Don't be like that—it's just food. Join me and Simona." The way Hassan said this made me feel like I was being melodramatic.

I looked at Hassan and saw that kind smile of his. "Are we going straight to the restaurant, no stops?" I asked.

He gave me a wounded look.

"Fine," I said, caving in and hating myself for it, "let's go eat."

CHAPTER 31.
Exit Emmanuel

EMMANUEL WAS STANDING BY a window. The curtains were open, and splashes of the late-afternoon sun drenched the room with light that was too bright. Pauline entered the suite and was immediately distracted by the temperature. She shouted, "It's like a bloody furnace in here! Close those curtains and turn on the fan, you dunce!"

Emmanuel snapped to attention for a moment, straightening himself and looking at her with unfocused eyes. He rubbed his nose, as if it could bring him back to himself, but just as soon as he did, his body shifted slowly, involuntarily, back into a slumped, half-asleep state. She had seen this before, the unmistakable trancelike lethargy of someone on heroin.

Pauline couldn't stop herself. She went at him with full force, kicking him to the floor. She swung and swung and swung, cursing and crying and shouting, "How dare you do this! How dare you do this!"

When she explained it to me in hindsight, she said, "He betrayed me with this shit. He ruined himself, his closest friends. He had been drugging for more than a year. It caught up to him. Still, even now, I don't know where his mind was when he turned to this shit."

Pauline beat him unconscious. Then she went around the room looking for any stash of heroin, his works, and money. And then she left. She paid off another two nights at his hotel with his cash and asked someone to go up and change his towels in a few hours. She wanted to leave him cold, but she couldn't. She didn't have it in her. She wished him dead, yes, but not yet. She needed to find a place to stay for a few nights to think before she headed back to Rome.

After she located a hotel for herself, the first thing Pauline did was place a call to Hassan, who sucked his teeth and asked her if she wanted him to fly out. Maybe it was hearing Hassan's voice or maybe it was the physical release of having beaten Emmanuel that gave her clarity, but Pauline knew that there was an opportunity in this for her. She said, "You don't need to fly out here, but we might meet up in Spain to claim the spoils of war. I will let you know."

"Very well, then," Hassan said. "Mind that you don't unleash your anger on the beggars. They are annoying, but they have a place in our world, too."

Pauline gave Emmanuel a day to recoup and sought him out the following evening. He was sitting in the teashop across the street from his hotel. He saw her first and waved her down. It was not until they were sitting in his hotel room that Pauline studied him carefully. "Look at you, you filthy rat. I should beat you every day for the rest of your life for this shit."

Emmanuel was weakened and banged up pretty good, but he was still himself, and he meant to show her. He said, "You got the better of me, but I won't let it happen again. I will kill you, you understand?"

Pauline laughed. "I get it, you're a man. You are still a man. But you are weak. Fuck you! My fear is reserved for people I respect."

Emmanuel was in no position to make threats. Pauline reminded him, "The police came right to your front door." His people, his crew, were sitting in jail while he was high on drugs, but she was not visiting his darkened hotel room to rescue him or salvage any part of their friendship.

Pauline asked Emmanuel for a full account of his business: what was left and what the Spanish police might find. How intense was their investigation, and did it touch on her trade and the trade out of Nigeria, Uganda, and Kenya? Were his other businesses safe? Emmanuel answered too slowly for Pauline, so she started shouting at him to open his mouth.

"Wait, wait," he protested, holding up both of his hands and trying to stop her. "It's not like that." Emmanuel explained that the bust had had nothing to do with drugs; as it turned out, having too many "irons in the fire" was what had finally caught up with him. Jojo and two others had been arrested for trafficking six Nigerian girls into Spain. The police had been alerted a few months earlier, allegedly from a source in Nigeria, and had begun their investigation then. Jojo was being held for human smuggling.

Pauline had heard enough; she was not interested in what Emmanuel did beyond his drug business. She had no moral position on trafficking girls, moving guns, and whatever else, but she could not work with him—their partnership was over. She told him, "You owe me for my packages that never arrived. You hurt my business and could have hurt me. I can't accept that. I need reparations." She asked him to think about how he was going to repay her.

She listened to his promises of money and nearly two hundred kilograms of heroin, which was being held at one of his houses, that could serve as repayment. But Pauline wanted more than what Emmanuel was offering—she wanted him out of the way. She wanted his supply line, his clients, his market.

In the end, she wouldn't get the glory of dissolving Emmanuel's business. In response to the arrests of key members of his crew, and to the prospect of long-term police surveillance, his clients stayed away and took their drug buying elsewhere. Emmanuel had a choice: to make the business smaller or to get out, and eventually he went into semiretirement. Spain was his home—he was a legal resident there—but he went back to Nigeria, paid politicians who worked for the military dictatorship to bolster his oil business, and tamed (but did not fully control) his drug habit.

Pauline acquired his connections in Burma and, with newly forged partnerships with some of Emmanuel's old crew, supplied criminal gangs based in Europe—largely in Spain, Italy, and Greece—with the heroin and cocaine. When Pauline chopped up Emmanuel's weakened business like a disappointed thief dividing up the meager booty, Emmanuel made a few requests, most of which were about maintaining important relationships with certain business partners in Nigeria. He also asked Pauline to consider taking on Jojo after he got out of jail. She didn't want to at first, not only because she never liked him, but because Pauline didn't like the idea of employing Emmanuel's right-hand man. She had her own trusted people; she wasn't about to have Jojo poison what she had built. But as Jojo bided his time in a Spanish prison and Pauline went back and forth to Spain, she realized that she could use him. "But I was going to make him work harder than he ever did with Emmanuel," she had decided. To her surprise, Jojo proved himself and she came to rely on him heavily.

As Pauline's supply line grew and her market expanded, she created a more direct route to transit drugs from Southeast Asia to Africa by putting Emmanuel on her payroll, making use of his Nigerian connections. In this way, she cut Cousin Henry out of her business and built up a profitable smuggling operation that went from Burma and Thailand through Nigeria, Turkey, and Bulgaria and on to locations in western Europe.

Pauline's goal was to run drugs—simply to acquire them and transport them to other gangs in Europe, be they members of the Naples organized-crime network, the Camorra in Italy, Nigerian dealers in Ireland, or French-based drug syndicates.

She managed to traffic large shipments of raw or preprocessed drugs to groups that would handle whatever it was they did best: local distribution or street-level selling.

And things went well for Pauline. She bought property in Uganda, a house in Nigeria, an apartment in London, three cars in Rome. She told me, "I even bought a beach villa in Mombasa [Kenya] that I have never set foot in!" It was *almost* the life that she had wanted for herself. But for Pauline, almost was not good enough.

CHAPTER 32.
Waiting Rituals

DURING HER FIRST FEW days at Rebibbia, the only people who spoke to Mary were other inmates. They explained the daily life of the prison and tried to prepare her for the peculiar hardship of waiting.

"Forget about your life out there," one woman advised her. "If you focus on getting through each day, if you set your sights only on marking off your days, then being here will be less painful for you."

"No," said another woman. "Remember your family and the life you had before you came—it might not have been a bed of roses, but it's better than this place. If you think only about making it through the day, you will not improve your situation. Take their classes, read the Bible, learn."

Mary did not want to think about how to while away her time inside a cage. She still had not seen or spoken to an attorney. She was not sure if she was going to go to trial or if the evidence that the police had found in her luggage was enough to lock her up and throw away the key.

Until now, Mary had never had occasion to think about differing justice systems between Italy and Liberia or even Nigeria, but to her—based on her experience waiting for a translator, waiting for charges to be pressed, waiting for a court date, waiting for a hearing, and waiting for a sentence—all the waiting in an Italian prison seemed to be just about as bad as anything that she could have imagined happening in Africa.

It would take Mary nearly six months to receive her sentence of six years. Apparently, she was lucky. She didn't have to wait nearly as long as many others who were being held by the Italian legal system. According to several human-rights groups, including Human Rights Watch, throughout the 1990s and well into the 2000s, Italy had excessively long pretrial detentions in which those whose first hearing in court was pending could wait an average of nine months to a year, and during that time were held in general prison populations under extremely crowded conditions. This was especially the case for foreign nationals, who often had to wait long periods for one of the limited number of English-speaking criminal defense lawyers or translators to become available.

When Mary realized that there was a very good chance that she would, in fact, experience a winter in Rome, she began to pay more attention to her surroundings. In the months since she had come to Rebibbia, she had noticed how the prison was divided. The Italian women kept mostly to themselves, and, of course, because they were imprisoned closer to home, they seemed to be better adjusted to life inside. They knew the unspoken rules, the cultural codes, and how to get things done. The girls from other countries—Latin America, Africa, Asia—formed little groups based on language, nationality, regional proximity, and, for the handful of Muslim women, religious affinity.

Mary understood why this was the case, and she had no desire to change the way things were done in prison. But she knew that in order to help herself, she had to learn how to navigate the waters on her own, and that required accepting that she was going to be in Rebibbia—and, by extension, Italy. She was stuck and hated the feeling of being mute. With limited courtroom and legal translators and even fewer English speakers in Rebibbia (except several of the other foreign detainees), Mary knew that she had to learn to navigate the system all on her own. So she embarked on a new routine: studying Italian. It was the only other task that she performed besides her ritual letter-writing campaign to her children. Writing letters to them was the only way she could continue to feel that a small part of her was still alive. Every evening, after mopping the prison corridors or washing dishes in the kitchen, Mary would take a stack of old folded newspapers and place them on the floor of her cell. She then sat on this pile of newspapers and wrote out her letters on borrowed or bought pieces of paper.

She tried to keep her letters happy, but she did not lie to her children, as some of the women in Rebibbia did.

Unlike the other women, she could not tell Peter and Jacob that she had decided to stay in Italy, that she had a good job at a factory, and that she was saving money for them to come join her. A lie might have eased their minds, allowed them to sleep more easily at night, thinking that someday they would all be in Italy together. And perhaps the boys would have even comforted themselves with stories of living in a big house in Rome or attending school here, and dreamed of no longer being refugees. Mary wished she could give them all of that in real life, and it killed her that she couldn't.

"My children were orphans," she would say to me. "They lived in a church building; they slept on a mat on the floor. Why would I willingly fill their hearts with poison? Besides, my sons have lost so much, seen so much; surely, the idea that I left them to care for themselves while I lived high in another country would be a betrayal." She shook her head at the thought.

"Besides," she added, "they are all that I have left in the world. They are the only two people who know me, my name, my country. My children are *me;* they are James. I am their mother, and this is a love that is too difficult to describe. That I would ever willingly abandon them . . . " Mary stopped herself from imagining the kind of person she would be to do such a thing.

So each night, Mary wrote a detailed letter to her sons about her life in prison and how much she missed them, and how sorry she was, and how much she wished that she could turn back the clock and make different choices. She placed each letter in an envelope and addressed it to the church. And every morning, she sent the envelope off to the post with a silent prayer that her letter would reach her boys and find them safe and healthy. And every afternoon for six years, she awaited their reply.

CHAPTER 33.

Becoming Boss

THE FIRST TIME PAULINE noticed that she wasn't feeling well was when she was on a trip to London. She had brought the kids—she wasn't sure why, but she supposed it was mostly because they were old enough to look after themselves. She was at a meeting with her Ghanaian friends, a rowdy pack of male relatives from a wealthy Lebanese family. "Oh, they used to make me laugh!" she recalled fondly. "I always called them my African brothers, because I never met any black people— Africans—who were so ashamed of being African! It was always 'Lebanese this' and 'Lebanese that.' And they were born and bred right there in Accra. Never set foot in Lebanon and probably couldn't even find it on a map!"

Despite their African roots, the Lebanese lived in London. They helped Pauline launder money—that was their trade. They were wrapping up a long lunch at a quiet pub, when Pauline noticed a thick gold watch on the wrist of the younger cousin. Pauline asked him where he had gotten it.

"At a jewelry store," he replied.

"I know that, you idiot. I'm asking you *where,* as in which store, what's the address, where the fuck did you get it!" Pauline didn't realize that she'd raised her voice. She began to sweat.

Her Lebanese friend looked at her, confused, but told her without hesitation that it came from the shop of his friend, and that he would be happy to take her there if she liked. The offer calmed her; pleased, she said, "Let's go there after we leave here. I like that watch. I think it would look good on my wrist."

Perhaps it was the way she said it or the fact that they had been drinking a little, but the men at the table, including Hassan, who traveled everywhere with Pauline, burst into laughter. Pauline's rage gathered slowly at her feet and worked its way up her legs. The weight of it made her feel as if she were going to fall over, and she started to rock back and forth. One of the Lebanese quickly stepped in with an explanation, trying to make her see what was so funny to them. "It's a men's watch," he said, and threw out, "It's supposed to be a Rolex, but we think it's a fake."

Pauline didn't hear anything beyond the first word of his sentence; she started shouting, "Don't you laugh at me!" She didn't remember, but Hassan would tell her later that she then threw glasses and plates and anything else she could get her hands on. Hassan pulled her out of the pub, her children running behind them, until they reached the car.

He took them to the apartment and left Pauline in her bedroom, where she lay sweating and shivering, both hot and cold. Her behavior was baffling. Yes, she had a temper and was even prone to what some might call fits of rage—everyone around her knew that—but she was never like this. Pauline preferred to direct her fury at specific targets; her anger was never random and always had some underlining purpose. She showed force to make a point: "In my experience, people respond to physical threats. If someone thinks that you can and will maim or harm them, well, they don't delay giving you what you want."

It wasn't just that she had acted so irrationally; she also felt that something was wrong with her—she was physically unwell. The fact that she heard her daughter, Isabel, answer the phone and explain to Hassan, who had called to check in, "Ma is lying down sick" seemed to confirm it all the more.

PAULINE TRIED TO AVOID any conversation with Hassan about what had happened with the Lebanese. Alone and still feeling unwell, she set out one day in London to make things right. She stopped in a Rolex store and bought a watch. She paid too much, but she considered it a high-stupidity tax. Her outburst with the Lebanese could hurt her credibility, damage her reputation, ruin her business. She sent the watch on to the young man she had lost her temper with. "These guys—they were the next level. I needed them—they were very good at what they did, among the best."

Pauline's cash volume was high and growing. She had outgrown her own in-house methods of laundering cash, and one in particular, which involved using several bank accounts under different names in different countries—what's called "smurfing"—was starting to lose its effectiveness.

In the beginning, Pauline, Hassan, her old friend Dora (the Kenyan woman who had introduced her to Bresnik), and a Spanish girl, Claudia, had made deposits in banks throughout Rome and, later, in other banks in Italy and London. Their deposits were small, as they were in cash, and often they had to exchange their money first from U.S. dollars to lire and British pounds. It was too tedious for Pauline, so she made Charles quit his studies to take over handling the money. By then, her husband had all but given up trying to lead his own life. Pauline had become more brooding and violent, and her demands for his time had increased, as she always needed him to do one thing or another for her. He picked up small envelopes from men in cafés, messengered dates and times to Moroccan men playing football on a grassy field, and met a young Spanish couple at the train station. No one told him, and he didn't ask, the purposes of his duties. He just performed them and tried to hide himself away, in the library, a park, with his children, with his friends—anywhere away from Pauline.

Charles didn't need to ask any questions, because he already knew about the business. Pauline made no effort to hide it from him or the children. Still, they didn't talk about the details—that is, until she sat him down one day when he returned from the library. She didn't waste any time.

"You're not blind," she started off. "Where do you think all of this comes from?" She motioned with her hand to their new furniture, the sofa that he was sitting on, the television, the loafers on his feet.

"I know you sell drugs," he said. "I think even our neighbors know that."

"Is that so?" Pauline was amused by the thought. She never brought her business home with her—only Hassan had ever been to the flat, and she had introduced him to her neighbors as her brother. They lived in a small building with two apartments on each floor. The building housed one other African family—Somalis who had been in Italy so long that Pauline thought of them as white—and the rest of Pauline's neighbors were Italian: a single working mother with her adolescent son, an older couple who owned the dry-cleaning business down the street, and two elderly Italian sisters and their yappy little dogs.

"Sure, they know," Charles said. "If they don't think you're a drug dealer, then surely they think you're a prostitute. You're always around strange men, men who are not your husband. How do you think it makes me look?"

Pauline was near howling with laughter at the thought. She may have even wiped away a few tears, she was laughing so hard.

"Oh, Charles," she said when she finally caught her breath, "I pity you. I never knew you cared. And you shouldn't, because you are hardly a man! Always behind a damned book, instead of working! How must it look to others, knowing that your wife slaves away all day working while her husband plays schoolboy for ten years running?"

Then Pauline grew serious. She took Charles by the collar and told him that he was going to start working. He had to earn his keep or get thrown out onto the streets—let his family in Uganda take care of him like a baby if that was what he wanted. But if he was going to eat her food, sleep in her apartment, take her money, then he was going to work for her full-time, with a set job description and set pay. It was time for him to stop being her errand boy.

Charles protested; he didn't want to sell drugs. He didn't want to go to prison or be shot or have to carry a gun. Looking back on this conversation still made Pauline laugh. "Charles was smart at book learning, but he didn't know real life. He thought I was living some American film, like *Boyz n the Hood* or something. He was scared. I understood that. He was weak in his nature, you know; he couldn't change that."

Pauline had shown Charles the door, given him the opportunity to leave if he wanted to, but he had stayed, she said, because despite his moral objections to drugs and his fear of arrest, he liked the money too much.

But Pauline didn't really want to bring Charles into the smuggling life. She laughed at his violence-fueled fantasies of cops and gangsters, but the truth was that things were heating up and drug trafficking was getting more difficult. It wasn't just that the police's powers of detection were improving and transit routes were being compromised; it was also that Pauline faced more competition and the increasing demands of the corrupt officials whom she had to keep up with. And, perhaps most dangerously, her own insatiable need, her greed for more wealth and more control, were becoming a problem. Pauline wanted to secure her future. She thought she could buy herself a nice, bland existence, retire into a legitimate trade, become a developer back in Kampala, pump money back into her country, be a pillar in her community, and even open a trade school for girls.

The money that she already made just wasn't enough, and soon she found herself losing cargo and three of her men in France, due to a police raid. Next, her crew became embroiled in some arrests in Spain and in a turf war with a Nigerian gang that left one man dead in Bangkok

Then she got a warning from the Italians—a courtesy call from her former employers—that she was getting too big. The fight with the Nigerians, she could handle; she knew who was behind them and had a sense of the size of their operation. But the Italians were tricky. She moved drugs for them, and her history with them was long. But how much did they really need her? She wasn't sure. Luckily for Pauline, the Italians were having problems of their own—anti-Mafia crackdowns and infighting were keeping them busy.

Under all this noise, Pauline knew that she needed more hands. She had little time to think, and that was clearly what she needed to do at this point. "I had to come up with a plan. But every day there was something—travel, or this or that. I needed to strategize." She had seen this all before, with Emmanuel, with others: the easy distractions that came with expansion, the logistical hassles of more money, the increased risks that people in the business were prone to take because of that place inside them that demanded that they keep pushing.

In other words, Pauline knew that she was on a collision course, but she could not stop herself. She had made an earlier promise to keep her children—whom she did love, though they might never know it—safely out of the way of this mess. After all, she would say to herself time and again, she was doing this in large part for them, so that they could choose whatever life path they wanted, so that they could study and have opportunities and make a name for themselves.

In a way, Pauline wanted Charles to steer clear of this business, so that if something happened to her, the children would have him to look after them. But she also needed him—he was constant and predictable. So when she brought him to her office, a small apartment in Dora's building, Hassan looked at her as if she had gone mad. "Not now," she said, as she pushed Charles past him and steered him into the back bedroom.

Sitting next to an electronic money counter was Claudia, smoking and talking with Jojo.

"This is Charles," she told them. "He is doing our books. He stays with the cash."

CHAPTER 34.

Dust of Living

I WAS COMING HOME from spending time at my favorite bookstore. I wanted to walk, but it was February and cold. I was in Trastevere, a warren of tiny streets that I loved to get lost in. With the arrival of winter, I had found myself without a warm place to go. Because I spent most of my days at the prison, I began to hate being inside any room that wasn't bright and spacious. My apartment did not meet those requirements, and besides, it was never a place of quiet serenity, anyway. And since it was cold, Villa Ada, my favorite park, was no longer an option. So I found myself hopping on a bus and walking over the Tiber River to get to Bibli, the bookstore that had become my home away from home.

As I was walking along my usual route, I passed a bus stop. A crowd of people started to form, all of them eager to jostle their way onto the bus in hopes of nabbing the last seat.

Just looking at the gathering made me tired. But I decided to join them.

When one bus came, people poured into it as others tried to squeeze their way out. I decided to wait for the next one. I had no idea where any of the buses were going, but I knew that they were all heading in the general direction of the central train station, so I wouldn't get lost. I had to laugh at myself. I had lived in Rome for a year, and still I treated the city as if I had arrived just two weeks ago. My daily life was so consumed by my research that I spent time only in places no tourist would ever want to see: police stations, prisons, dirty bars, run-down apartments, random half-empty buildings on the outskirts of the city.

Hassan had become my tour guide to the Roman underworld. But because I did not have a strong sense of where anything was in Rome—though I could always tell you which direction Rebibbia was—I never remembered where any of the places were that Hassan had shown me. If I were to meet him and Jojo at any public location, like the Wimpy's of our very first meeting, I usually had to leave two hours ahead of schedule. It was just enough time to take the wrong bus, ask several people for directions, backtrack, and get to my meeting on time.

The next bus to approach was half full. I took it as a good sign and got on. I made my way to the back, where I was hoping to find a seat. I spotted one and kept my eyes trained on it, as a way of claiming it before anyone else sat in it. It wasn't until I sat down that I saw Albert. He didn't look much different from the last time I'd seen him that day in front of the optical shop talking to his friend on the scooter, but it had been four months and his hair was slightly longer. He had seen me get on—I could tell by the way he sat up stiffly, turning his face away from mine. My heart was racing; I restrained myself from speaking. I had promised him I would leave him alone. So I did. I took a book out of my bag and tried to read. Two stops later, the bus was nearly full. An elderly Italian woman got on the bus, and I moved to let her have my seat.

"No, let her have my seat," I heard Albert say. He was out of my line of vision, blocked behind two people. I then heard him guide the old woman to him, and I turned to see his hand reach out and gently take her by the arm. And then he was standing next to me. "You haven't turned the page since you got on the bus," he remarked.

"Yeah," I said, "I guess I'm a slow reader." I knew I was going to have to get off the bus soon. "How have you been?" I asked. I figured I wasn't breaking any rules, since he'd spoken to me first.

"Good, thanks. I noticed that you stopped following me."

"Yeah . . . sorry about that," I said, ashamed all over again. The bus stopped. I was going to have to get off soon; otherwise, I was going to get very lost. Albert watched me looking around.

"You getting off?" he asked.

"Next stop," I replied. I started to put my book away and tighten the belt around my jacket.

"Why did you want to speak to me? I thought you were a maniac or something." We both laughed.

I quickly explained to him that I had been doing research at Rebibbia and interviewing his mother. "She doesn't know that I have met you, and I would never tell her. Believe me, I think we both know that your mother would do nothing but pressure me to get you to come see her. I don't want to be put in that position, and I'm sure you don't want that, either."

Albert nodded. "Has she unleashed her dogs on you yet?"

I looked at him, not sure how I was going to answer. The bus was slowing down. I started to stand up. "You mean Hassan and Jojo?"

"Those guys. Others. For someone who is supposed to be under twenty-four-hour surveillance, my mother is a remarkably free woman." He moved out of the way so I could move toward the door. "You still have my number?" I nodded. "Call me in the afternoon. I am going to the cinema with friends. You can come along and meet my girlfriend."

I jumped off the bus and started backtracking toward a familiar monument. I wasn't sure what had brought on his change of heart, but I was glad that I had run into Albert—and genuinely excited that I would get a chance to speak to him about Pauline. But I was mostly looking forward to an evening at the movies. I was happy for the first time since I had moved to Rome.

CHAPTER 35.

Diagnosis

"IT'S GETTING TOO HOT out there," Jojo said, but he wasn't referring to the temperature outside. The problems with the Nigerians were getting more complicated, and the day before, Pauline had lost a load of heroin in Bulgaria, and no one had yet heard from the drivers. Pauline suspected theft, but she would have to wait and see if the driver made contact with their handlers. In the meantime, she had to figure out the logistics of her latest shipment—a large one that wasn't being transported in her usual way.

She had gone in on a deal with an associate in Nigeria. They had agreed to use couriers on commercial flights as well as a few private planes. It was not the first time Pauline had used this method, but this deal was going to involve three different airports, seven different countries, and upwards of 150 people, and would be spread out over two or three days.

When Pauline recounted this story, I estimated that she was going to move about three hundred kilograms, more than six hundred pounds, of either cocaine or heroin or a mixture of both. The street value of this amount of drugs in the 1990s would be about $50 or $60 million if it were coke; if it were heroin, it would be about $240 million. Either way, the shipment stood to be the largest single gain for Pauline yet.

What she hated the most about using couriers was the sheer fact that they were people, rather than cargo holds of the boats and private airplanes that she normally used. "And people," Pauline would say, "always make mistakes." She didn't take drug losses in stride. Losing any amount of drugs, even if it was only four kilos, was four kilos that she could not earn money from. But that was the nature of the business.

Getting drugs out of an airport was not usually an issue, anyway—especially if they were departing from locations where Pauline had "relationships": Lagos, Dakar, Casablanca, Nigeria, Senegal, and Morocco. The couriers—what we commonly call drug mules—would be on flights heading to France, Spain, Italy, and Germany. She had crews ready to meet people in each location, just as she had people—customs officials, screeners, janitors, and even employees of fast-food chains inside the airports—working for her, although they didn't know it, as their only direct contact was with whoever their handlers were.

Jojo was the highest-ranked member of Pauline's crew who had anything to do with lower-level operatives. He generally recruited handlers, who either hired other people who hired drivers, couriers, and others in turn, or hired them outright themselves. Pauline had a quiet respect for Jojo; he was never bothered by getting too close to the action. From convincing someone to swallow, carry, drive, or fly heroin or cocaine someplace to passing through airport security with money or drugs strapped to his body, Jojo liked the challenge; in fact, he claimed he was more often bored by the ease with which he could pass through undetected. Pauline's crew weren't all like that. But she, Hassan, Jojo, and a couple of others always did what they had to do—even if it meant driving a shipment of drugs over the border or carrying a kilo or two onto a plane, none of them was above doing what was required for business. Though they took every precaution not to get caught or robbed by others, this business was unpredictable, and Pauline admitted, she found that exhilarating.

But Pauline was distancing herself from all of it—not because she was having any kind of moral crisis about it, but because she just couldn't trust herself. She was sick— or at least, she thought she was. Her outburst in London had turned out to be the first of many. She had become a screamer, as Hassan said to her once. The slightest thing could set her off—a perceived joke that she was not in on, a sideways glance from someone around her, or an answer not given quickly enough. She had taken swings at just about everyone around her and fought with people on the street, in restaurants, and in shops; once, she had threatened to kill her neighbor's dogs.

Hassan had taken it upon himself to act as a buffer between Pauline and others. He kept her calm. He urged her to go to see a doctor. He was worried, and pointed out how bad she looked. One day he stood her in front of a mirror. "Look at you," he said. "You are sweating, your eyes are yellow, and you are losing weight. You are acting like a lunatic, calling me at all hours of the night and trying to kill the *vecchios* for crossing the road too slowly. You need help. Go see a doctor."

Pauline knew he was right. Something was clearly wrong. She was sweating a lot—too much. At night, if she managed to fall asleep, she would wake up bathed in sweat—it didn't matter what the temperature was, she could be sweating and shivering at the same time. A few weeks after her outburst in London, she found herself spending her nights in her bathroom, showering and then, after dressing, thinking, planning, and pacing the floor in her living room.

She used to call Hassan in those moments, wanting him to sign on to some scheme or another. And at first light, she would start rousing her crew. She could sense that she was pushing them too far, demanding too much of them. They avoided her if they could, moving into separate rooms when she entered the one they were in, running off to do an errand when she came through the front door of the office. The more they avoided her, the more she pushed herself on them. Slowly, she grew suspicious of them. Why were Jojo, Claudia, Patrick, Mathew, and even Dora acting so cagey? she would ask Hassan.

Pauline would not tell Hassan, but she had already seen a doctor when she was in London. He had listened to her symptoms and offered her two explanations: menopause or stress. "Get out of here!" she had answered, even though she was in his office. "You are telling me this so you can send me away without giving me any treatment. How convenient." She had left his office thoroughly convinced that all doctors were the world's best-educated fools.

But Hassan wanted to drag her to a fellow he had seen two years earlier, for a problem that he had never named. When he finally stopped asking one day and just drove her to the doctor's office one afternoon, Pauline decided to stop putting up a fight. The doctor was young and seemed to know Hassan well. It was strange for her to be in a situation in which Hassan was the one in charge; he was never afraid of Pauline, and for the most part they were equals, but there were always subtle ways in which he would defer to her so that others around them would know that she was the boss.

Pauline didn't mind this doctor, but she wasn't happy with his diagnosis, either. He ran some tests and suggested that she might be hypoglycemic, though she had never had diabetes. The test results would give the doctor more answers, but the best-case scenario, if Pauline was hypoglycemic, was that she needed to eat more or take medication; at worst, she would have to have part of her pancreas removed.

Hassan seemed unmoved by the news; he told the doctor, "Give her something to help her sleep. And something for during the day—something to balance her nerves."

Pauline had heard enough. "I won't take it, so put it away." With everything that was going on, she thought it might actually be good not to sleep. Moreover, she needed a clear mind and had to stay alert. Pauline knew that one of her rivals, sooner rather than later, would make good on his threats.

CHAPTER 36.

Salutations from Sunny Nigeria!

IT WAS UNEXPECTED. BUT when Mary first held the envelope from Nigeria in her hands, she had a sinking feeling that something was not quite right. It had been eight months since she had arrived in Rebibbia. She wasn't quite used to being in prison, but at least now she was finally able to sleep for a few hours every night. She was also cordial with all the other women, though she hadn't made friends with any of them.

When Mary saw the letter lying on her cot when she returned from her work in the kitchen, she thought one of the other women had misplaced the envelope. Then she saw her name on it in unfamiliar handwriting.

Despite her ominous feelings, she sat down and tore the letter open eagerly. It was a short letter, less than a page long.

The first line revealed who the sender was. Her hands were shaking almost uncontrollably. Her eyes scanned the lines, though the words did not penetrate her mind. But she did not have to understand the contents of the letter intellectually, because she already knew the meaning of the words in her heart. This was the letter she had been waiting for, the one that would explain why after so many months she had still not heard from Peter and Jacob, her sons.

Eddie had tracked her down. In her darkest hours, her fear that he would harm her children was an evil that she prayed he was not capable of. The thought had terrorized her when she had first arrived, but it had slowly faded away as she made up countless excuses for why she had not heard a word from her children. But this letter, a letter from Eddie, forced her back to the terrifying reality of her situation: With no friends or relatives in Nigeria whom she could contact to protect her young children, she was at the mercy of a powerful man who was accustomed to using and deceiving people for his own gain.

When Mary showed me the letter, I was struck by how nonchalant Eddie was. It was everything that it should not have been—friendly, reasonable, and vague, and because of that, chilling. I read it and copied it down:

Dearest Mary,

Salutations from Sunny Nigeria! I have received your frequent letters and am informed of your stay in Rome, the capital of Italy. My brothers

*and I were disappointed that your journey did not
conclude in Lagos with your parcels safely in hand.
Consequently, much money has been lost but [we]
have conscripted your sons, fine, growing boys, to
lend us a hand in the repayment. Upon your return
you may settle any outstanding debit, rest assured.*

Best Wishes.
Sincerely,
Eddie

When I first asked Mary if I might see Eddie's letter
sometime, I thought that, despite the years that had passed, it
might contain some piece of information that could lead to her
children. In the weeks between the day she told me about the
letter and the day I actually got to read it, I fantasized about
finding a missing clue that would direct me to Nigeria, where
I would organize a team of police who would surround Eddie's
criminal complex in some nameless town there. I stayed awake
well into the night, envisioning myself kicking down Eddie's
door and scooping up Mary's children, all the while shouting
at the police, "Arrest that man!" As Eddie tried to escape their
clutches, he would confess to everything and, in doing so, allow Mary to go free. Then she would fly back to Nigeria to be
reunited with her sons and head off to lead a normal life in
exile in a country of her choosing.

I wanted these things to happen for Mary—actually
longed for them to—but not because I saw myself as a savior

in any sense (or at least not consciously). Mary might not have needed me or anyone else to rescue her, but she did need either a miracle or justice. And I was well aware that I could offer neither. Still, Mary had become my friend, and beyond that, she was alone in the world.

CHAPTER 37.
Respect

PAULINE HAD TURNED TO her books. She studied up on General Patton, read about the Mau Mau rebellions, got her hands on speeches from Mussolini, learned about Carlos the Jackal and the Red Brigade, and was inspired by Machiavelli's *The Prince*. To her face, Hassan lauded her efforts, though Pauline was beginning to suspect that he found her reading tastes amusing. But that was not all she was suspicious of.

Pauline thought that she was being followed. It had to be the Italians—maybe even the police. The prospect of surveillance, and of possibly being under investigation, pushed her dangerously close to the edge. Her health seemed to be worsening by the day: She was losing weight, her skin had taken on a slack, ashen look, and she was sweating so much that she had to carry two changes of clothes. But still, she did not go back to Hassan's doctor; she claimed that she didn't have time. They were moving ahead with the run out of Lagos and Dakar in less than a week. Her associates in Nigeria were getting restless. They were having some problems with officials in the military, over payment for patrolling the warehouse where the drugs were being held.

Pauline decided that she needed to train her crew according to some of the military strategies that she was reading up on. She started holding meetings with Hassan, Jojo, Charles, Claudia, and the Nigerian brothers Patrick and Mathew. At first they indulged her. But when she suggested that they all start acquiring weapons, they began to protest: Mathew told Pauline that "gun violence brought gun violence," and Claudia, who had just started working the recruitment angle and had spent much of the past three weeks cajoling people—unemployed or underemployed young people, mostly women and students— didn't think she needed to carry a gun to any of these meetings. Besides, Jojo, her longtime boyfriend, did carry one, so she felt like she was safe. Charles didn't say anything, but then, he didn't need to—his face registered his dismay.

"Listen to me," Pauline warned them. "They—somebody, I don't know who—are coming for us, so we have to be prepared." She knew that she sounded paranoid, but she believed it to be true. Reflecting on the announcement from her prison cell in Rebibbia, Pauline could see that the warning had been strange, but at the time she had felt the need to protect herself. She recalled, "I wanted to control what I could. Never before had I been so weak; I had no strength. I didn't like the limita-tions of illness. Weak people bring out pity in some people and hatred in others. I saw the looks of the people around me, and they gave me both. So I tried to show that I was strong, here and here." She pointed to her head and her heart.

Privately, Hassan told Pauline that if they started to col-lect guns, the nature of their business would change, and he didn't think she would want that. But she wasn't interested in hearing any words of warning or sage advice from him this time. Hassan and Jojo carried weapons. Pauline was also no stranger to guns, having owned a few since her days with Bresnik.

But Hassan knew her well, and he pressed on. He told her that he understood that she was feeling the pressures of the latest shipment—there was a lot at stake. It was an "All-African Summit," as Jojo had called it. They were working with a large Nigerian syndicate, along with some smaller crews based in Senegal, Morocco, and Europe. It was a lot to coordinate—anything could go wrong, Hassan acknowledged. But it was foolhardy to start thinking about weaponry now.

For Pauline, getting guns—Hassan had rightly as-sumed—was not just about self-protection; it was about self-preservation. She was looking for a way to move the business into other areas—areas that the Italians might appreciate. "My thinking at the time," she told me, "was that I wasn't ready to leave Rome in a box. I knew that moving guns in and around Africa was easy. If we went in this direction, I could do it from my front porch in Mombasa." But Hassan—who had taken part in weapons deals in the past and had worked as a mercenary soldier for a brief time after his student days—claimed that she and their crew were not ready for something like that.

"You are not required to play the part of a mobster," he said. "I see you read these books. I listen to you quote from them. Why? We are not at war. We are not soldiers, and you are not a general. We are in business. We move drugs. We sell them and we make money—that is what we do."

Hassan also told Pauline in no uncertain terms that she needed to do two things: get herself well and focus on the business at hand. "I have stayed with you longer than I have wanted to because you are a good friend, you are smart, and we have done well. But now it seems you have lost your senses!"

When Pauline heard his words, she thought of her many conversations with Emmanuel that were similar, if not in tone, then certainly in content. The only difference was that she cared for Emmanuel in a different way than the way in which Hassan cared for her. Hassan was her comrade, her teacher, her student, and her brother. Emmanuel was an infatuation first, a business partner second, but they were never friends. Relationships like her and Emmanuel's were bound to fade once they had outlived their usefulness. But friendships like Hassan's didn't just disappear; they only got more complicated.

"What does Machiavelli say?" Pauline asked me rhetorically. "That when everyone can tell you the truth, you lose their respect."

CHAPTER 38.
Metamorphosis

"ACCOMPANY ME TO THE airport," said the voice on the other line when I answered the phone.

"Who is this?" I asked. And then I heard the confident, rich laughter. Hassan. "It's a bit late, don't you think?" I asked him.

"It's not even seven thirty," he said. "Come with me to the airport. It's a long drive, but I promise you will be back home and fast asleep by ten o'clock."

"Come on, Hassan, please. I really don't want to go to the airport. It might only be seven thirty, but I'm tired." I also had made a rule that I was never going to meet up with Hassan or Jojo past dark. For some reason, I believed that during the day I was safer, that I would be less likely to find myself in the middle of a drug buy, or if there were a police raid, my claim to being an anthropologist doing fieldwork would somehow sound a lot less dubious.

"Listen, my nieces are flying in from Holland. Come meet them with me. I need you to. They are young women. They will like you. Me? I am just their old uncle; they see me all the time and are bored with me. Besides, you have to say yes. I am just downstairs in my car."

I hated that Hassan was so charming and persuasive. I hated that I was so easily swayed. I'm not sure whether I lacked the conviction to stand by promises that I made to myself or if I just allowed myself to be controlled. But there had always been a part of my personality that was all about surrendering. And in my twenties, I mistook capitulation as a form of opening myself up to life experiences. I hardly ever said no to a request, especially if it seemed easy to fulfill. And a trip to the airport seemed simple enough. So, without taking the time to really think about it, I gathered up my jacket and house keys.

HASSAN AND I RODE to the airport in silence. I watched, mesmerized, as the sky turned from dark gray to black. I fell into my own thoughts. Going to the airport made me think about going back to the United States, and I realized that I was not ready to leave Italy, not yet. There were so many places that I still hadn't seen. I had never been to Venice, for example, I had spent only two afternoons in Florence, and I had yet to see the catacombs of Rome.

"What are you thinking about, beetle?" Hassan asked. I looked at him for a moment, taken aback by his choice of nicknames. He focused on the road ahead of him.

A momentary image of a beetle flashed in my mind. Beetles were ugly; some even looked like roaches. *How is calling someone a beetle at all flattering?* I asked myself. Instead I answered, "I am thinking about Kafka. *The Metamorphosis."* It was a bad attempt at a joke, but I figured Hassan would at least at smile at my effort.

"Ah, a wonderful story." His eyes were on the road, but his face, his furrowed brows, the way his voice sounded hollow and distant, all indicated that he was preoccupied. Even if he'd had any interest in what I was really thinking, I wouldn't have told him. Because what I really wanted to say was that I was worried that when I looked back on my time in Rome ten or fifteen years later, I would regret that I spent so much of my time going back and forth between prisons and tagging along with drug smugglers.

The Rome that I was living in was not the Rome of other people's postcards. While I wasn't looking to be dazzled by a prepackaged presentation of the city, I was becoming painfully aware that I was missing out on much of its beauty, its culture. For example, I had never walked along the Appian Way. In fact, I had never really thought about walking along that road before I'd gotten into Hassan's car, but I suddenly had the urge to now. I stared out the window. We were getting close to Fiumicino. I could see the lights of the airport.

"Do your nieces live in Holland?" I asked.

"What? Oh . . . " Hassan hesitated. "No."

I waited for him to tell me more.

He turned and looked at me briefly. "They live in Paris with their mother. My sister, Saarah."

I nodded my head. I had heard of her. But I kept looking at Hassan. I couldn't figure him out. He was a willing interview subject. He spared little detail when it came to talking about his past and his relationship with Pauline. He had told me just enough about life in Sudan, his childhood, his student days, and living in exile in Europe to make me feel like I knew him, but in fact I knew nothing about who he was in the present moment. I didn't even know what part of Rome he lived in. I didn't know if he was married or if he had children. And now he was driving me to meet his sister's daughters.

If Hassan was a friend (and I wasn't sure he was), then his friendship was one of circumstance. He was like a co-worker at a temp job whom I would have lunch with every day, but no matter how much we confided in each other, we would never really be friends beyond the parameters of work.

I wasn't sure when this particular job for me was going to end, but I knew that when I left Rome, I was probably not going to see or speak to Hassan again. And I was pretty confident that he felt the same way about me. So I was suspicious about his motives for taking me to the airport. When he had called, and the whole time I had been riding in the car, I had been having doubts about this trip. In a way, though, I didn't care. I may not have wanted to participate in anything that would be illegal, but there was a part of me that didn't shy away from the idea of witnessing, maybe from a safe distance, an illegal transaction. I told myself that I had seen enough drug deals just by walking through Washington Square Park in New York City on a weekday evening to immunize myself against the notion that illicit activities took place only in the shadows of everyday life.

"So, do your nieces work for you?" I wanted to cut to the chase, get it out in the open. Stop pretending.

"Work for me?" Hassan burst into laughter. "You mean, do they have kilos of opiates in their hand-carry?"

I shrugged. He laughed some more. "Asale!" he chastened. "Please, this is my family you are talking about. Do you really think that I am such an ogre?"

I didn't say anything, and we sat in silence. Hassan might have been slightly indignant, but still I didn't believe him. He didn't speak to me until we pulled into a parking space at the airport.

"Listen." Hassan was solemn. He turned his whole upper body around to face me. "I don't blame you for asking. I may be a common crook and even a vile person, but I am not that person every day of the week. I don't like or dislike what I do to make money. It just is. I smuggle drugs. In some countries it is illegal; in other countries the politicians all get their cut. It is all about perception. The biggest drug smuggler in the world was Queen Victoria. Did she worry about the effects of opium addiction on thousands of Chinese, or the enslavement of poor Indians as they cultivated that opium?"

He looked at me. I wasn't sure if he expected me to respond, so I said nothing.

"Sometimes I do think that I am horrible—a monster, really—when I think of what I am putting out into the world. I have lived a long time and I have done many, many things in my life—some good and some bad. I am human. And I am no longer surprised at what humans will do, out of fear, or out of greed, or out of necessity. One way or another, each of us signs a contract with the devil—some of us are just more obvious about it. You know, I wasn't born a bad guy. And I hope I don't die one."

Hassan pulled the keys out of the ignition and smiled in a slightly conspiratorial way as he continued, "By the way, did Pauline ever tell you that she lived in England before moving to Rome?"

"No," I said.

"Oh, yes, that is actually where we met. She was in nursing, you know."

"Nursing, really?" I had a hard time picturing Pauline caring for the sick or the wounded.

Hassan nodded his head, noting my disbelief. "Yes, really. She was not exactly saving people's lives, but she was attending to the elderly. She was very good with them. Tender. It was lovely to watch her work. Her patients adored her."

"That's amazing," I said. "Honestly, I'm shocked."

"But that is my point." Hassan took my arm, guiding me toward the arrivals hall. "Just because you meet someone in a cage does not mean that they're an animal. It's like our friend

Gregor [the main character in Kafka's *The Metamorphosis*]: He may have turned into a bug, but that did not make him any less a man."

CHAPTER 39.
All-African Summit

THE FIRST DAY OF the All-African Summit went off without a hitch. Pauline and the members of the other Nigerian group that was partnering with her each had a few different handlers working airports in France and Germany. On the second day, twelve of her people did not get on the plane leaving from Lagos, and four were arrested when they got off the Casablanca flight. On the third day, everything went wrong. Her handlers in Rome—two Tunisian men and a Pakistani man—did not make contact with couriers. Pauline sent Mathew to the airport to see what was going on.

When she got the call from Jojo, who was in Morocco, that nearly all of the couriers her team had recruited to fly out of Lagos and on to Casablanca had not arrived in Morocco,

Pauline knew it was more than a coincidence. "Get Samson over here now!" she shouted to Patrick. To Hassan she said, "I am going to kill that son of a bitch, and then we are getting on a plane and we are going to kill every one of those bastards! You don't think this is a war? What the hell kind of double-cross is this? They're dead!"

Pauline's mobile phone was ringing. Soon Hassan's phone was ringing. She picked up hers and threw it against the wall; upon contact, it exploded into tiny plastic shards. Charles had come out of the small back bedroom to see what was the matter. Pauline stood in the small galley kitchen of their office apartment and turned over a little table, scattering the sugar bowl and breaking a jar of instant coffee. She was so preoccupied with her rage that she didn't notice that Hassan had left to answer his phone.

The call was from Nigeria. It was the number-three guy of Gabriel, the man who headed up the crew in Nigeria that Pauline was partnering with. "It's D," the caller said. Hassan had met him twice and spoken to him often over the past couple of weeks. He knew his voice.

"What happened?" Hassan asked.

"Look, man, it all changed. We go tomorrow. Portugal. Paris."

"You couldn't tell us this for six hours? Does Franklin know?" Hassan was referring to his man on the ground in Lagos.

"Man, I don't know. He should. I talked to him today."

Hassan was irritated. Worse than D's seeming indifference was the fact that he kept saying "man." Hassan was a creature of formality; he respected all languages. Shortcuts, lazy or indirect speech were high on his list of annoyances. "Have Gabriel call me on this number."

Hassan hung up the phone and went back to the kitchen, where he found Pauline leaning over the counter. Charles was bent over the floor, cleaning up the mess she had made in her rage. He told Pauline everything D had told him. "We need to get ahold of Franklin, now. We need to get ahold of people in Paris and see who we know in Lisbon. If it's all right with you, I would like to deal with Gabriel myself."

When Pauline had first told Hassan that she had struck a deal to work with Gabriel, he had thought it was a bad idea. It wasn't that differing or even potentially rival networks didn't work together—they often did, but not like this. Instead of each crew's taking on a specific task, the magnitude of this shipment required that each organization involved pool its resources: recruiters, handlers, couriers, drivers, ground contacts, police, and other officials. What happened was that each group worked in concert to flood the channels at the various airports they used, knowing that officials could pull, at most, only three or four couriers from the hundreds of flights that came in each day.

To date, the record number of drug couriers caught on a single flight was twenty-three; in December 2001, these people had been arrested on a randomly searched Air Jamaica flight from Kingston to London Heathrow. A week before that, nineteen couriers had been pulled off a flight from Kingston to London Gatwick.

And in the days before September 11, Pauline and the other African syndicates involved knew that from a law-enforcement perspective, it would be unusual for a coalition of traffickers to pick the same day (or the same three consecutive days) and the same destinations to transport drugs to. The problem, Hassan told me, was that there had been a tacit agreement that certain flights "belonged" to the various crews, meaning that the drugs on each of those flights and the money attached to them were tied to individual groups. In Hassan's view, this was an unnecessary vulnerability.

"Why not agree to take the total amount of the shipment and give each crew a percentage of that total amount, based on the percentage they put in?" Hassan argued to Pauline. But none of the groups could agree on exactly what should come to them, so they decided that they would treat the run almost as if it were like any other import-export, meaning that the volume of drugs each crew could transport determined the size of their profit. They would then pay a percentage of the anticipated profit to the supplier.

Then Hassan asked Pauline the next logical question: Why couldn't they just buy the drugs outright, as they would from any other supplier, and move them on a date and time they chose? Her response, he recalled, was simply "It's political."

"It didn't make sense to me," he remembered thinking. "Why all this trust among crooks?" In Pauline's day, it was a well-known fact in different circles, from law-enforcement agencies to traffickers themselves, that African drug syndicates usually did not succumb to the same threats—internal violence, gang rivalries, and even drug use among the opera-tives—that other groups, from Mexico, Colombia, Italy, and Brazil, among others, usually encountered. This was not to say that there was never any violence or turf wars, but the com-mon perception was that West African groups in particular were focused mainly on their bottom line and had neither the energy nor the resources to waste on displays of power unless they were absolutely necessary. So perhaps Pauline and the other syndicates thought they had little to worry about if they participated in the All-African Summit, but Hassan was more skeptical—and precisely what he had feared would happen did.

Mathew went to the airport, where he met up with Ali, one of the handlers. They looked around—despite the fact that they knew no one had come off the flight—and then went to the drop house, a flat that drug couriers, after arriving in their destination city, go to (sometimes alone, sometimes with other couriers or with a handler) to deliver drugs.

They found Hamdi and Mourad sitting in the flat. Ali and Hamdi told Patrick the same story—that Samson had ap-proached them at the airport and told them that there had been a change. They had called Mathew, and then Hamdi had come to the drop house to tell Mourad.

Mathew and Patrick were confused. Samson did not work directly for their crew—he was one of Gabriel's men, and Pauline and her crew had known him for several years. But these three guys wouldn't know him. Only Patrick, Mathew, Claudia, and Jojo worked directly with handlers in Italy and

Spain. Mathew hadn't finished telling Pauline the story when Hassan got the call from Patrick that he was with Samson.

"What do you want me to do with him?" Patrick asked over the line; Hassan repeated the question aloud so that Pauline could hear.

"Take him to the building," Pauline said, referring to a dilapidated building outside of Rome that had once been a bakery, or at least held baking equipment. Pauline sometimes used the building to warehouse drugs for a day or two before shipping them off to clients; it wasn't especially large, but it was freestanding, was on a quiet road, and never drew any interest from anyone. Pauline paid a group of immigrant workers who lived in a small house right outside the fenced driveway, a kilometer or so away, to keep an eye on the place.

Before Pauline walked out of the house, she grabbed the gun that she kept in a box in an armoire by the door. As she was halfway out the door, she spotted a bag of clothes that Charles had brought in with him. She motioned with her head to Hassan. "Bring that," she said, and went out to the car.

CHAPTER 40.

Underneath Oblivion

IT WASN'T A LIMP. It was more like Mary's right leg was detached from the rest of her body. All of her determination was contained in her left shoulder; it steered her toward me. I stood up when I saw her, shocked by her transformation. It had been only a matter of weeks since I had last seen her, but she had aged significantly in that time. Her short hair was pulled back into her customary small, tight bun. She had tried to carefully comb her hair over the large balding patches on the top and sides of her scalp. For the first time, I saw little sprouts of wiry white curls at her temples. I moved around the desk to meet her halfway.

"Please." Her voice wavered. "I can do this. Let me do this." She tried to smile. Her jaw was clenched tightly. Her lips were gray and drawn back over her teeth. She had lost some weight in her face. Her cheeks were hollow. The skin hung slack around her mouth.

I stepped away from her and moved back toward my chair. I stood with my hand on the back of it, secretly hoping that my grip would somehow give her more stability. I felt helpless as she dragged her right leg slowly across the room. She was so focused on making it to the chair next to mine that her eyes were trained on it as if to make sure it didn't move.

In the last letter I had received from her, she had told me that she had slipped, for the second time, while doing her job as a cook in the prison's kitchen. This time, the fall had made her old injury worse. What she hadn't mentioned was how much pain she was in, or that in order to recover, she would need a surgery that she would never receive, because the prison would not pay for it.

Mary finally made it to the chair and slumped down in it. The armpits of her white T-shirt were wet with sweat. On the front, oil spots streaked down the middle. She had on dirty green track pants. "I know," she said, looking up at me, "I don't look too pretty."

"No, you look fine," I lied, trying to reassure myself more than I was her. I sat down quickly and tried to distract myself by turning the pages of my notepad.

"Come on," Mary said with some disgust, "I'm not blind or dumb, and neither are you." She sat with her right leg extended out in front of her. She rubbed it up and down with long strokes.

I looked up at her. She was not angry with me, but I knew she was not someone who was easily charmed. "Okay, yeah," I admitted, "you look like you're in a lot of pain."

Still rubbing her leg, she let out a rueful laugh. "I am. Did you receive my letter?"

"About the accident, yes, I did. I'm sorry I didn't write back, but I knew I was coming to see you today."

"It's all right, you will send me a hearty letter some other day." She switched gears to talk about her injury. "Since the day of my fall, I have not seen a doctor. They won't allow it. They want to wait another week to see if I am really suffering or just trying to get out of work. Can you believe these people?"

I shook my head in disbelief. I didn't know what to say.

She was still rubbing her leg absentmindedly. "Whenever the administration hears a rumor that there are drugs in a ward, they come into each cell and tear the room apart. Never mind if you are known for not taking drugs."

I looked at her, confused. "Did they suspect *you* of having drugs?"

Mary shook her head. "I don't think so, but I am not sure. Maybe they think another girl in my cell or in my section had drugs. But when they came into my cell and pulled everything apart, I didn't mind, because it is a common practice when they search, so it was all right. But the guard, when she came out of my cell, she was carrying my pillow. She said that she would have to write me up because I had an extra pillow. Now, I tell you, sister, I didn't care about the write-up, but I need that pillow—a doctor gave it to me after the first fall I had. I use it for my leg." Mary looked at me with pleading eyes.

"You have to understand, I never cried so much as I cried for that pillow. I begged the guard. I was on the floor. I put my self-respect in the waste bin. I didn't care. Two other guards came and pulled me up off the floor. By then I was screaming, really begging! They took the pillow anyway, and they wrote me up for my behavior.

"It's a pillow. They won't even allow me a second pillow." Mary's eyes looked wet; tears were starting to form. "I despise these Italians here, you know. After they took that pillow away, I thought that I would never show them my weakness again." She stopped rubbing her leg and looked at me with determination. It was a look I had not seen before—a hard, cruel gaze. "This place is changing me. I told myself that they couldn't reach my heart, but they are getting in slowly. They are turning me to rot."

We sat silently for a while. I wasn't sure why, but I felt like Mary was slipping from me, as if she were going to go away from here. I decided to tell her that I was worried.

"Why?" she asked, with a slight smile on her face. "I am not going anywhere. Believe me."

"I know," I said, "but something is wrong. You don't seem like yourself."

She thought for a moment, considering, I presumed, how she might reply. "I am not sure what is going to happen to me in here, but I want you to know something—if you don't hear from me for a while, don't get worried." She waited to see if I understood what she was saying, but I didn't.

"What's going on?" I asked, bothered that she was being so cryptic. "What happened?"

"Listen, you are my sister and I support your studies, but I have asked you before to stay away from that woman." I didn't have to ask Mary which woman she meant. She had cautioned me the first time to keep my distance from Pauline, back when I hardly knew either of them; then she had kept on with the warnings in her letters and in our interviews, and sometimes even passed through the mouths of other women I spoke with.

I couldn't tell her about meeting Hassan and Jojo. Nor could I say anything about my fears that I was being drafted into Pauline's service and that I was starting to feel morally compromised. I didn't want to tell Mary that I thought she was right, that I wished I had stayed away. In a sense, I think she already knew.

"She is wicked, and you will end up hurt or in trouble. I know you better than you think I do. I see how you are, Asale, and I also know what it is like to be your age. When someone, anyone—me or Pauline or Joy—asks you to do something, you say yes straight away without thinking about what it might cost you. Even when you want to say no, you say yes. I can see your regret."

I nodded my head. I knew that if I opened my mouth, I would confess my misgivings about Pauline, tell Mary what I had seen.

She sighed. "I will tell you why I lost my pillow—why my cell was raided in the first place. Because Pauline told someone here in the prison that I had drugs. And why did she tell them that? Because I told her that she needed to stay away from you. I told her that I knew all about the way she works. She was angry, and so was I."

I was growing nervous. Pauline was not one to be confronted. Everyone knew that—her temper was just too unpredictable. "Did the two of you fight? Did she hit you or something?" I asked.

Mary chuckled. "No, thanks be to God! If she had hit me, I would not be sitting here right now. I would be in the infirmary."

"And you are sure that Pauline started a rumor that you had drugs?" While I didn't put it past Pauline to do something malicious, she was usually more up front with her retaliation. Something as passive as starting a rumor seemed out of character for her.

"No. I am not sure. But she has many friends, you know; she is in her element with a lot of these crooked women here, and I don't mean just the prisoners. The guards and administration, they can all be bought."

I thought about what Albert had said, about how his mother was still working the trade from the prison.

"Go home," Mary said to me. "And if you don't hear anything about me, don't be troubled. I promise that I will write to you the moment I can." She stood slowly and with great care. "And don't come here looking for me. Let me tell you when you can come and see me."

"Okay." My imagination conjured up two scenarios: that Mary would try to escape or that she would try to kill Pauline.

"And sis," she added, "stay away from Pauline. Don't end up on the wrong side of this wall."

I helped steady her and led her to the door. She hugged me long and hard. It was the last time I ever saw her.

CHAPTER 41.
Guarded Privacies

WHEN TWO OF MY letters to Mary went unanswered, I tried not to panic. I went back to Rebibbia but did not see her, for the first time since I had met her. And I kept waiting for someone to tell me something, because I had promised Mary that I wouldn't ask about her. Finally, one day I spoke with a Nigerian woman named Christina, one of the many African inmates Mary had helped by translating and filing requests or educating them about court procedures and prison rules when they first arrived at Rebibbia, like she had, plucked from the airport and brought straight to the prison, not speaking a lick of Italian.

Christina seemed shocked that I didn't know. "I am so sorry, Asale," she apologized. "If I would have known, I would have told you sooner. She is being reproved."

"Reproved?" I was confused. I knew what the term meant, but I wasn't sure what it meant in the context of prison. Most of the time, the women I spoke with used Italian words or phrases when discussing legal aspects of their case. So when they were talking about their court proceedings, they would say *processo,* and when they were talking about an early-release program, they would use the term the Italian officials used: *semi-liberta.* But I knew that for Christina, who had not had the opportunity to go to secondary school, the term "reproved" was an English approximation of an Italian legal term.

"What does that mean? Is it bad?" I asked her.

"Yes. She was written up, and now she goes back to court."

Christina told me that Mary had been written up for drugs. And because she had been accused of a serious offense, even if they had not found any evidence, she would have to be put under investigation. She must have lost her privileges, and she certainly could not receive any visitors. Until she was cleared, whatever parole date or early- or work-release plans that she might have set up for herself would be called into question. Prison officials could decide to extend her sentence if they wanted to.

I thought of the warning Mary had given me the last time we had seen each other. She had said that Pauline would come after her in some way. In my mind, her being written up for drugs had all the indicators of a Pauline payback. I was aware that Pauline had spoken often to women I had interviewed, and suddenly I knew I needed to protect both Mary and Christina. So I changed the subject. "What is your favorite music?" I asked Christina lamely.

As she talked excitedly about different groups, my fear that Pauline or someone else might have asked the women I had interviewed what and whom we spoke about came back to haunt me. My anxiety about what happened after I left the prison each day had immobilized me for months when I had first started working in Rebibbia. Now, I had come to realize that in order to do the work, I had to push my worries aside while still taking as many precautions as necessary.

Since I conducted all my interviews in English, I came to know which guards and prison administrators spoke it. I kept two separate notebooks: one that I carried to the prison, which I wrote in using a code, and one that I transcribed my interviews in at night and whose pages I would tear out and send to my grandmother for safekeeping the next day. And just in case anyone other than the intended recipients read them, I always kept my letters to the inmates lighthearted or asked only about their lives before prison. And I never spoke with the other women the way I did with Mary. She was the only person who talked to me candidly about her thoughts on the various prison officials, Pauline, and some of the Mafia women who were held in the facility. She was the only one who told me about the brutal police abuses, the late-night beatings of women—mostly foreign women, African women—whom police picked up off the streets for prostitution and brought into Rebibbia, then beat them, maybe even raped them, and sometimes sent them back out onto the streets the next day.

She told me about the Romani women and girls who were held on minor charges—petty theft, purse snatching, or begging—and placed in cells, beaten and violated by having their hair, which is an important cultural symbol in their community, cut off. Sometimes the police would cut the braids, weaves, or long hair off the African girls, too. For Mary, the hair cutting was crueler than the beatings.

CHAPTER 42.

So Gentle a Woman

IT WAS A TYPICALLY beautiful summer night. The sun had set hours ago, but the air remained warm. Still, Pauline was shivering slightly. Excited, nervous, pissed off . . . the combination of those emotions pumped adrenaline quickly into her body. She was out of the car and walking up to the back of the building before Hassan could even stop fully. Pauline stood at the door and waited for him to catch up with her before they made their entrance.

"Got the bag?" she asked him.

He held it up in front of her in response. They went inside. Patrick and Samson sat on a couple of folding chairs, smoking and talking casually. When Samson saw her, he stood and extended his hand. Patrick had already gotten up and walked to the other side of the room, pacing near the door that led out to the front of the building.

Pauline didn't reach for his hand. "Sit down," she ordered. Samson looked at Hassan, not with any trace of worry, but with a look that Hassan read as embarrassment, perhaps—not so much for himself for being snubbed, but for Pauline's lack of grace.

"Samson was an elegant man," Hassan told me. "He was very well educated, not just in letters, but in class. He had such decorum that when he was in a room, people seemed to mind their manners so as not to offend. I liked that about him. He was a person to be admired."

Samson merely nodded his head in response to Pauline's behavior. Given the circumstances, he felt that there was not much for them to say.

Pauline sat next to Samson and asked, "What happened?"

"Didn't Gabriel tell you?" The fact that Samson was answering a question with a question made Pauline even more suspicious.

"What happened?" Pauline asked again, this time with more force.

Samson claimed that in Lagos, someone higher up in the government had gotten wind that a few ranking officers were patrolling a large cache of drugs and stood to make a significant sum of money. The officers went to Gabriel and put pressure on him to give them a cut of the profits; otherwise, they were going to shut down the operation.

Gabriel had wisely removed some of the drugs, shipping them off to various points within the city and sending them on to the border of Benin in anticipation of headaches with the military after the initial hassles he had received. The real problem, Samson revealed, was that many of the drugs had been brought in by the police perhaps, or government officials, or a combination of both—from a neighboring country that had obtained the drugs in two recent seizures. Gabriel was concerned that if officials in the Nigerian government or the military found out that the drug purchase had come from across the border, they would "tax" him more than they already did, or, more likely, they would confiscate his cargo and sell it back to him or someone else.

The goal for Gabriel was to keep the process—his connection, the routes—as covert as possible so that a gang more powerful than he was could not steal his trade right out from underneath him using his same techniques. Gabriel thought that such a gang would be made up of members within the military dictatorship of Sani Abacha.

Pauline listened to all of this with interest, trying to assess the truth of Samson's words. It was feasible, she would admit, that everything he said was true. She had been working with Nigerians in and around the country for a very long time, and everyone knew that the government, as she put it, "were the biggest mobsters in the region." It didn't matter from one government official to the next; under Sani Abacha, Pauline told me, "even us—the legitimate mobsters—were often appalled at their audacity."

Pauline's perception matched reality. Abacha, a military man and a former minister of defense, was the tenth president of Nigeria (1993–98) and famously brought international sanctions against the country for annulling the 1993 elections (after claiming that he would finally allow democracy in Nigeria following successive years of military dictatorships). Also under Abacha, Nigeria faced sanctions because the country failed to bring its counter-narcotics effort into alignment with international standards.

Abacha's criminal "audacity" placed Nigeria at the very top of Transparency International's list of most corrupt nations in 1996 and 1997. Abacha is considered one of the top five most corrupt world leaders (behind Zaire's Mobutu Sese Seko), having embezzled $2 to $5 billion from the country.

PAULINE WATCHED SAMSON'S FACE to see if there were any subtle signs of dishonesty: nervous gestures, sweating, little eye contact. Samson displayed none of these traits. On the contrary, he seemed confident and relaxed as he laid out for her what had transpired next: The crew on the ground in Lagos managed to get the drugs off the first day, as planned. The second day, they knew they would not be so lucky, so they shifted some of the couriers to fly out of another airport in Abjua, and they got the rest of the drugs they had in their possession out of the country; they were going to try to salvage as much of the operation as possible. "We should all know more in the next day or two," Samson said when he was done recounting what had happened.

"Why didn't Gabriel call me?" It was Pauline's turn to talk, and all she had were questions. "Why didn't *you* call me?

Instead you went directly to my guys and told them there was a drop, and all the while I am sitting here, waiting for my cargo! You made me look like a fool! You tell me this story and I am supposed to walk away from you and hope that I get the rest of my shit?"

"My apologies, Pauline. I know that this is highly unsatisfactory," Samson replied.

"Highly unsatisfactory?" Pauline repeated, scoffing at his understatement. "The only way your apology means anything to me is if it comes in a bag with $4 million in it. All you are offering me now are excuses."

"I misspoke," Samson agreed. "We will make you whole. But for now we must all be patient."

Pauline was tired of Samson's mannered voice of reason. She found it condescending. She began shouting, "Don't you instruct me, you asshole! I don't work for you, remember? I don't work for Gabriel and I don't work for you! You assholes work for me! I am your client!"

Pauline knew that Patrick was watching her, waiting for a signal to jump into action. What kind of action, she didn't really know at the time. Her mind couldn't really focus on that at that moment. She was busy replaying everything that had happened—comparing what Samson had told her with the actual events of the last two days. She wanted to move past the truth that not getting her shipment was "highly unsatisfactory," and the circumstances highly unusual, but she couldn't. She had worked with Gabriel before, and there had never been a problem—sure, some minor glitches, but nothing like this.

She had made a major investment in this run; she had staked lots of money up front to cover the logistics of moving a high volume of people and drugs. She had rented cars and houses and had already paid out bribes and airline tickets, and now all that money was gone—no refunds, no returns.

Did she trust Gabriel enough to hope that Samson was right, that in a few days she would get some of her drugs back? Maybe, but there were too many holes. Franklin, her man in Lagos, hadn't checked in yet. It wasn't like him. And she knew that any of her people would have stayed with the drugs and kept her updated on the situation. None of this sat well with Pauline.

She walked over to Hassan. "Take the clothes and get him dressed. Meet me in the car. We're going up the road." Hassan nodded, without saying a word or looking at her.

"Okay, Samson," Pauline heard Hassan say as she went outside, "put these on."

PAULINE WAITED IN THE car, staring out at the sky. It was blue-black, and there were just a handful of stars. Somehow the sky felt heavy, as if weighing down the whole world. She saw Samson walking between Hassan and Patrick. "Shit," she muttered to herself. Samson was wearing Albert's soccer jersey and shorts. *Why did Hassan have to give him those clothes?* she wondered. But it was too late to do anything.

She started up the car, and the three of them got in the back. If Samson was scared, he didn't show it. He didn't speak, and he just stared straight ahead. Perhaps, Pauline and Hassan each speculated separately to me, he would not have liked making a spectacle of himself, so he chose not to make a fuss.

Pauline drove until they saw an old, darkened villa that had long ago fallen into abandoned disrepair. When they turned into the driveway, Pauline saw the flash of African women in wrappers running off after their men, who, because they were undocumented immigrants, had taken to the fields, fearing that the car's headlights belonged to the police. She pulled up close to the house and cut the lights. Nobody needed to say, "Get out." They just followed Pauline as she navigated her way around the trash piles that ringed the villa like sandbag barriers.

When they had walked a little past the house, out toward the fields where the immigrants had run off to, Pauline stopped. Hassan and Patrick brought Samson in front of Pauline. She considered him for a moment, standing with his back against the heavy black sky. He should have looked tiny and vulnerable against it, but he didn't. He stood straight, almost rigid. Pauline thought he resembled a little general about to command an army that included her. Even in Albert's football gear, he looked dignified. Except for his shoes. They were out of place. They were expensive black wingtips that belonged on the feet of someone walking into a boardroom.

"Take off your shoes," Pauline ordered. Samson hesitated for a moment. He started to bend, and as he did, he let out a long, annoyed sigh. Pauline got the message: This— the indignity of standing in shorts, a T-shirt, and bare feet in the middle of a garbage heap—was the worst thing she could possibly do to him. He was humiliated. Now he knew how she felt.

"You can run along now," Pauline said, prepared to take the humiliation one step further.

But Samson knew what was coming. "No," he said simply, "I will stand right here, if you don't mind."

Pauline shrugged—she told me she remembered that detail because it was a gesture that she never liked, but that her children used frequently. Samson was standing not more than three feet from her. *Close. Messy,* she told herself. Her gun was already in her hand. The weight of it pulled her shoulder down so that she stood lopsided, leaning to one side. She held the gun out in front of her, surprised in a way because her arm felt like a spaghetti noodle. In her ear she heard the voice of her Uncle Kefa, who had taught her everything, including how to shoot birds and rats with his military revolver, say, *Hold steady. A quick, clean shot.* Pauline did not look at Samson's face. She didn't look at anything. One minute, she set her eyes on the target, and the next, she pulled the trigger in a blur.

Samson didn't fall to his knees or straight back with his feet in the air. To Pauline's surprise, he sort of gently sat down; a look of bewildered curiosity came over him. He looked down at where the bullet had entered and let out a strange-sounding laugh. Pauline told me, "It was haunting, his laugh—it was almost like he was laughing at himself. What else can I say? It was a very private moment for him. He discovered that he was human."

Pauline walked away. Hassan or Patrick—she did not know who and would never ask—did what she could not. The sound of the second gunshot tore through the air, so rattling Pauline that she nearly stumbled onto the ground.

When she got back to the car, she could not steady her hands. When she recounted this story, she told me, "My hands were shaking, but I had presence of mind. I was not hysterical, nor was I sad or scared or worried. In that moment, my only thought was that it was such a shame that Samson was wearing my son's clothes."

CHAPTER 43.
Out of Time

I WAS GROWING INCREASINGLY worried about Mary. All of my letters had gone unanswered. To keep myself busy, I made my dreaded return to the male prison to talk to men in the drug trade. I was unhappy about going back to the men's ward, but it was more easily accessible than the women's prison, where prison officials, Maria the *educatora,* and several of the guards made no effort to hide their displeasure whenever I came around.

I had tried to stay out of their way and had never made any requests other than to come back the following week. But even that was getting impossible. My most recent request had been "lost," so I had been required to go back to the minister of justice to gain permission to enter the facility again. I had faxed my original request letter to the minister—the one my friend Stefano had helped me write—so many times that I had to keep it in a protective plastic sleeve because the paper was breaking down. It could be a matter of days or a matter of weeks before I would get the call from the press office giving me the okay to use their original letter again to present my case to the prison.

It was a bureaucratic game that I hated playing—a useless exercise in the display of power. Going to the men's prison, Rebibbia Maschile, was an insurance policy. I had no trouble getting in there—they were used to outsiders and had a strong sense of public relations.

Conducting research, for me, had migrated. It was akin to starting out collecting butterflies, then moving on to all winged insects, then finally to general bug ephemera. If there was even the smallest chain that linked prison, Africa, and drug smuggling, I was all over it. I was looking for the answer to one simple question: Why did people go into this trade in the first place?

I had learned from women that there were many reasons, some more insidious than others. Some had no choice—they were desperate to feed their families—and a few, like Mary, had no idea what they were carrying. Other women, like Pauline, saw the drug trade as an out—a quick, though dangerous, way to have a more expansive life. I knew about the women, but I didn't understand if the motivation for men was any different. Yet going to the male prison did nothing to make me feel any closer to the elusive truth of the drug-trafficking world. I was trying to burn up my days and fill my calendar, so that I could tell myself I was being productive. But really, I just wanted to go home.

I returned to Rebibbia Maschile with trepidation. Frankly, I wasn't sure if I could stomach any more men telling me how they had "punished" the women around them. I entered the male prison with a bitter taste in my mouth and a clear set of rules when I spoke to each inmate: Don't tell me about any violence against women, I would say. Putting some conditions on my interviews was limiting and probably contradicted the advice of professional interviewers everywhere, but I didn't care. I was killing time, waiting for my permission to come through from the minister of justice so that I could get back to the women's prison. I did not hide the fact that my loyalties lay with that ward.

All this was on my mind when I made my third visit to the male prison. I was so used to the strictures of the female prison that I found that I generally liked walking through the men's ward. Unlike in the women's section, I had freedom to roam around designated areas. As I walked along the corridors— the arteries connecting all the cellblocks—I would pass a guard every now and then, and, even more rarely, an inmate. The guards would greet me with a nod or not acknowledge me at all. And despite the annoying habit of one guard, who thought it was cute and clever to shout out, "*Ciao,* Whitney Houston, *Americana!*" every time I passed him, I felt official, professional, and even grown up—none of the things I experienced when I worked in the women's section. It boosted my confidence.

On that particular day, I went to section G8. I didn't have any person in mind that I wanted to speak to, but I knew that Patrick, from Pauline's crew, was held in that ward. I had interviewed Patrick before. He was long-winded and pedantic and spoke like a television lawyer. He re-created every story as if he were delivering the closing arguments on *Law & Order*. Still, I found him engrossing and effective.

Besides Patrick, there was the old inmate who ran the small, crumbling matriculation office at the entrance of the cellblock, a bookish man who remembered me from previous visits and welcomed me with kindness. He called for Patrick over a phone that looked as if it had been made at the start of the twentieth century.

"Wait right here, please." He spoke to me gently in Italian.

I stood inside the cellblock, just outside the matriculation office, facing the barred doors that led to the inmates' cells. The room was huge and had only one exit, the same barred gate that I had just entered through. I leaned against one of the windows and put my notebook down on the windowsill. I waited for Patrick, figuring that I had called on him while he was working his prison job. I had expected him to come through the door that led to the inmates' cells, so I was surprised when I saw him walk over from the cellblock entrance.

"Hey-eh, my friend!" Patrick called to me. He was walking over with two other men. One man was, like Patrick, Nigerian. I had seen him before. The other man was Colombian. We had not met.

"Hello!" I called out. "Do you have time to talk today?"

The three men walked over to me. Patrick made brief introductions. "Oh, bad timing, friend. We are off to lunch. Come back after—" Patrick's voice was drowned out by the sounds of shouting and scuffling coming down the hallway from the cells. Soon, a single guard rushed through the door, followed by several men who were fighting each other. The cacophony of yelling and the dull thud of fists on flesh filled the room instantly. In the crush of men, Patrick and his friends stepped in front of me, shielding me from the mayhem.

Then, just as soon as it had started, it all seemed to end. Prison guards pushed through the main cellblock gate. I couldn't see how they subdued the men, but they used something—batons or other heavy objects. The sound was that of paper being crumpled, sharp cracking followed by a hollow, distant echo. And the room went still. The voice of authority flooded the space, angry, threatening, loud. I couldn't understand what the captain was screaming at the inmates, but the men seemed to evaporate. As they vanished quickly from the room, Patrick and his friends stepped away from me, leaving me exposed. My eyes fell on a man writhing on the floor; he was lying on his stomach, trying to stand up, using his head as leverage. The sight of his face both disgusted and saddened me: It was shiny with sweat and blood, his skin already swelling on one side, distorting his eyes, nose, and mouth.

The captain caught sight of me and bellowed at some guards to get me out of there. I heard him, but I didn't pay attention. I was too busy trying to catalog the scene in front of me: one man, with blood all down the front of his shirt, being held up by some prison guards; another leaning against the window across the room, moaning in pain, his arm hanging lifeless at his side.

A guard came up to me, reaching out his hand to grab me, but I stepped back. "Don't touch me!" I said in English. "I'll come on my own."

As I walked down the hallway with six guards in front of me and two guards behind me, the only thing I could think about was the overused line by Robert Burns: "Man's inhumanity to man makes countless thousands mourn." But instead of hearing this as a dirge, I felt it pounding against my brain in an aggressive litany.

I followed the guards into a tiny room, where they sat me in a chair and encircled me. The captain stood in front of me. He was not a large man, but I remember him that way: a barrel chest, thick arms and legs, tall. He had dark hair and wore glasses, with frames that looked as if they belonged on an African dictator, which is to say that they seemed hopelessly outdated. They were big gold-wired spectacles that brought to mind the 1970s. I could not look him in the eyes, so I looked at his hat instead.

I had never been interrogated before, but I knew that was about to change. I sat straight up, full attention, my head like a satellite receiving signals. I was electrified—all of my nerves had been turned on full tilt. They asked me question after question, the same ones over and over again.

Who was I, where was I from, why was I at Rebibbia, was I with an organization, who gave me permission to be in the prison, what was my research about, why did I say that I was with an organization, did I work for the Nigerian consulate? It was relentless.

Not until the captain sat down on top of the desk in front of me did I realize that I was in a room with other furniture. I was growing weary, and so were the guards. But not the captain—he held our attention by asking me more questions, confusing my words, making me repeat answers in better Italian. Some of the guards started to peel away, move back to their posts in other parts of the prison.

It felt like two hours or more had passed. I grew wearier. I slumped in my chair, and my brain simply gave up trying to speak in Italian. I quit. I answered in English, which the remaining guards found amusing, as did the captain. After a while, the men chatted amongst themselves, making small talk. None of it related to my research and me.

Finally, I asked if I could leave. The captain considered me for a long moment and gave me a big smile. "You can leave whenever you like!" He made it seem as if I had needed only to ask. He walked me down the corridor and back out to the administrative wing of the prison. Energized by the prospect of leaving, I walked quickly toward the exit.

"Wait. Wait, *ragazza.*" The captain wouldn't let me go yet. "I want you to meet someone." Next to him appeared a well-coiffed man in his forties, Marco Maccari. "This is a student from America," the captain told him. Then the captain turned and asked me, "What is your name again?"

"*A che bello,*" said Maccari, after I introduced myself. He took my hand in a firm, cold grasp. He spoke eagerly in Italian. "American? Really? But you don't look like you are from America. Actually, you remind me of a girlfriend I had. She was from Guadalupe. Do you know Guadalupe?"

I pulled my hand away from his with a strong tug. "No," I said. "I don't know Guadalupe. I have never been there. Really, I should be going now."

Listen, *ragazza,* you come back tomorrow. We will set up interviews for you." the captain said.

"Okay. Okay. I will." I really didn't want to go back there again, but now I felt like I had to. If they set up interviews for me and I didn't show, I worried that they would call the minister and I would never get permission to return to the prison. I couldn't seem ungrateful. I gathered my documents and looked at the time. It had been nearly five hours since I had gone to see Patrick.

When I stepped out of the prison and onto the street, I looked at the long shadows that the buildings cast. It was almost four thirty.

"Good night!" someone called from behind me. I turned and saw Marco Maccari. He stood in a small patch of late-afternoon sun against the prison wall. He reminded me of a snake warming itself on a rock.

CHAPTER 44.
Disinheritance

ALBERT LEANED ACROSS THE table and removed a bag from the chair that was intended for me.

"You got lost didn't you?"

I nodded, feeling embarrassed. "I am so, so sorry," I said, starting into a long heartfelt apology full of self-deprecating remarks about my sense of direction.

Albert wouldn't have any of it. He nodded his head toward the chair, "Sit down, you are here now." He spoke with a mixture of annoyance and relief, "Let's eat something. We waited for you."

I looked at the woman sitting at the table with Albert. Actually, she had been the first person I noticed as I entered the pizzeria. I didn't want to stare at her when I came in but with Albert's use of the word "we" I felt like I had the permission to look at her openly, with curiosity and without the formality of strangers. Everything about her appearance was unexpected, yet I knew Sheila, at least in my mind. She was the sister of Samson, the man Pauline had killed.

Sheila watched me take my seat and gave me a shy smile. She was a bigger woman than I had imagined her to be, fatter, rounder. But her features, her eyes, nose, mouth, were small and delicate. She seemed to hold herself in, as if afraid that someone might step on her. However, as worried as she might have been about going unnoticed, she dressed, at least in an Italian context, in a way that drew attention to her. Which is to say that she wore a more traditional African outfit: a brightly colored matching shirt and skirt of yellow, blue, and green swirls. The sleeves of her shirt puffed out significantly, giving the effect of sandwiching her chest between two cushions. On top of her head was a beautifully knotted wrap. She could have been royalty. But she was uncomfortable and insecure, like a little kid forced to be dressed up for the first time.

I smiled at Sheila as Albert introduced us. "Nice to meet you," I said, unsure of what I should say next. There is no etiquette for meeting a person who knows that you speak to her brother's killer at least once a week. This was part of the reason why I was nearly an hour late—I hadn't known how to prepare for this meeting. I didn't know what was required of me. And then, of course, there was the thought that kept popping up that I probably knew more about Samson's last moments of his life than his own sister. I pushed this feeling aside for now. I suspected that Albert had brought the three of us together so that I could share all that I knew about the night of the murder, but I wasn't certain of his motives. I did know that if she asked, I would tell her everything.

I HAD HEARD AS much about Sheila as Albert could tell me. She was a married housewife who lived with her husband and children in Leicester, England. Her husband worked hard, two jobs in fact, sometimes three. Every few years the family spent a month back in Nigeria, where they had a house and land and planned to retire after the last of their children were safely tucked away at University. I knew that Albert revered Sheila, maybe had even come to idolize her over the year that he had gotten to know her. In his mind, Sheila was the mother that Pauline should have been. The immigrant story, the story of striving in Europe, cobbling together a solid, legal, middle- or lower middle-class existence was all that Albert had wanted for his parents.

Albert tried to cajole Sheila into ordering something from the menu. "You have never had pizza before?" He was playful, sweet. "I promise you will like it, maybe even more than rice!" He teased. Sheila smiled demurely, shaking her head at his suggestion. She spoke, but so quietly that I could not hear her. Her lips moved and then she smiled. Her eyes darted nervously around the room, looking out for anyone who might disapprove of her mild display of pleasure.

Sheila was at least twenty years older than me, but I felt like I was more experienced, or at least less shell-shocked by the world than her. But I was surprised that she seemed so innocent. I knew from Hassan that Sheila, like Samson, was a relative of Gabriel. The same Gabriel who allegedly ran drugs out of Nigeria and neighboring countries for his own complex organization that included an Eastern European ring and a Colombian cartel. And it was Gabriel who nearly caused Pauline to lose her business and he who was responsible for sending Samson to Rome, into the lion's den. I wondered how much of this, if any of it, Sheila knew.

WE FILLED OUR TIME before the food arrived with Albert making small talk about Sheila's children.

"How old is the youngest one now?" he asked, trying to draw her out of her shell. "Six or seven? And your daughter, she just won some prize at school, right? Science or English or something?"

Sheila would simply smile and nod. She was not interested in pinning down the details—it was enough for her that Albert was in the general vicinity of the truth. The food arrived and Albert and I ate in silence with Sheila looking on, politely declining our offers to share. Finally, he pushed his plate away from him and turned serious.

"Sheila is back in Rome trying to see if the police will hand over some of her brother's things. His clothing and a wedding ring." I already knew this, however. He had explained the reason for her visit to Rome earlier that morning over the phone when he'd called to ask me to meet them. "It's been shit—"Albert stopped and looked at Sheila apologetically. He searched for the right words, but stopped short, as if knowing that anything that he pulled from his vocabulary would be a monumental understatement.

He looked at me, unsatisfied, like a man who needed a whiskey but could only find a beer. "It has been difficult for her family. The police see this as another case of some poor African migrant who got in with the wrong people. They are treating Sheila like she is less than the speck of dirt on the bottom of their shoe. Like she should be happy that they didn't just throw his body out with the waste the very next day."

"What happened?" I asked Sheila, "After he was killed? Do you know?" I waited for what seemed to be a long time before she said anything. Her eyes were trained on the table and I had to lean in to hear her.

"Well," she breathed out slowly, hesitating. "I got a call. A man told me that my brother was dead in Rome and that I should expect a parcel with his wallet and watch in the post. Then he hung up."

I nodded. This sounded like something Hassan would do, or have someone do for him. I knew that Pauline would not have been so thoughtful.

She continued, "And then my eldest son spoke to my uncle."

"Gabriel?" I offered.

I could see her close her eyes at the mention of his name. She nodded her head and didn't speak for what seemed to be a few minutes. I looked at Albert and shook my head, quickly mouthing "sorry." He was impassive. He lifted his hand and lightly touched Sheila's wrist. He picked up where her story left off.

"Sheila and her son came down from England. They made arrangements and flew back to Nigeria. The way he died and even after, it was—"

"Humiliating," Sheila interjected.

"Humiliating," Albert repeated slowly, as if translating for me. "She had to burn his body. We are Africans. This isn't something that we do. You understand? They said there was no other way to get him home."

Albert rubbed his eyes and forehead and put his hand on Sheila's wrist. "You asked me, Asale, why it was that I finally gave up on my mother? Especially now after all this time. It's because she did this."

"But how did you two meet? How did you find out about Samson?" I asked.

"Sheila's son, Tunde, wrote to my father. He also wrote to my mother, but she didn't tell you that, did she? Anyway, my father told me about Tunde, and we met a few months later." I opened my mouth ready with my next question but Albert cut me off.

"Let me finish. After meeting Sheila and her family, I started to really see what my mother was doing, how far she would go. I begged Sheila for months to come with me to speak to my mother and Sheila finally said yes. It was very important for me." We both looked at Sheila who was watching Albert speak. He still had a protective hand on her wrist. If I didn't know it I would say that he was her son.

"So I brought Sheila in with me for a prison visit. And do you know the first words out of my mother's mouth were? She said, 'Don't you think she is a little old for you?'" Albert's voice cracked with emotion. "Can you imagine the disrespect? This woman, who killed the brother of the woman standing before her, and this is what she had to say?" Tears started streaming down Albert's cheeks. "I wanted to take a long knife and split myself open, take out my veins, you know, anything that came from that . . . woman. How could I call her my mother? How? She has never begged forgiveness not from me, or Sheila, or my father, or God. She is sick. You get me? Not right." He tapped his temple.

I looked over at Sheila who was weeping silently. She seemed to be crying for Albert. She knew better than I did certainly, what it meant for him to be a son who walks away from his mother. Albert had no more reason to believe, as he had for years, that his mother would ever change. He finally realized that if he was going to continue to be her son he would have to accept her for everything she was, including being a murderer.

Sheila started to get up from the table and Albert stood to help her. Together, they walked back to the bathrooms. When Albert returned his eyes were red and he forced a smile. But he kept watch on the restroom door, ready to escort Sheila back to our table.

"You know," he said without looking at me, "I love Sheila and her family. They should hate me. But instead they love me back. They care about me and ask about my studies.

They are like . . . a real family." He glanced at me quickly, as if to see if I was still paying attention.

"She may not seem like it, but she has more strength than anyone in this room. You want to know why? Because she made it work. She didn't take any shortcuts, even when she could have. Her family could have done what my mother did, sold drugs. They could have tied a noose around anybody's neck just to make a point." He tore his eyes away from the back of the restaurant long enough to glance at his watch. The bathroom door swung open and he started to stand.

"You know, my mother was always telling me that she did everything for my benefit, to help me through life. Do you know how that makes me feel? It's like I'm an accomplice in a thousand different murders. Because really, between the drugs and men like Samson, how many people has she killed?" Before I could answer he already had his back to me.

I watched as he eagerly walked to Sheila's side.

CHAPTER 45.

Seasons of Sun and Rain

PAULINE WAS WEAK AND lying in bed on the day of her arrest. Samson's shooting had taken its toll, and she had tumbled headlong into an illness that could not be named. She had all but stopped working, leaving Hassan in charge of daily operations and any overseas travel. Pauline had also left him to clean up the mess in Nigeria. They had lost money on the deal, a significant amount, and her supply was down. She estimated that it would take five months or longer to reestablish their business. And she knew she had to get her supply line out of Nigeria. It was time. Others, too, had moved to neighboring countries, attracted to even weaker infrastructures and the promise of even better returns.

It would take some time, but she would get herself back up and running. This was what Jojo and Hassan and the others around her all told her. Pauline wasn't sure if they were talking about the business or about her body. She didn't need reassurance, though—she needed something more: hope, passion, the will to fight.

"I didn't care anymore," Pauline recalled. "It wasn't like me to not give a damn, but I didn't. I was driving off a cliff and I did not give a damn to stop or slow down. I just kept on going. It reminded me of Emmanuel, you know, his last days. So I guess you could say that I saw it coming."

She didn't remember exactly how the police came into the apartment, but she thought the landlady had opened the door for them. They didn't knock, they just entered. Charles was home, making some tea, Albert was away at school, and they had recently sent Isabel to Kampala to stay with one of Charles's sisters. Pauline heard some feet shuffling and the sound of male voices asking Charles in Italian to state his name and show them his identification. She could tell from the sound of Charles's voice that he was scared. *He must be shaking,* she thought to herself, and decided that she had better get out of bed. She didn't figure that the police were at her house because of Samson, but it was possible. Anything was possible.

She had just managed to sit up at the edge of the bed, when an officer walked in. "He actually excused himself when he saw me. He even helped me stand. I looked that bad." Pauline smiled at the memory. The police took her and Charles into custody. She soon found out that their arrest was linked not to Samson but to a drug investigation that included an Italian couple she had known since the 1980s. She was no stranger to the Italian legal process, so when the police asked her a series of questions, relating mostly to what they referred to as her husband's drug dealing, it only reinforced her theory about police incompetence.

"It was clear to me that the *Carabinieri* had no idea what they were looking for. I figured they had rounded up a few midlevel Mafiosi and were trying to make something stick—like getting poor little Africans to sell their drugs. They must have pulled my prior arrest, and here I was, almost ten years later. What nonsense! I thought it would be only a matter of time before I was sent back home."

The evidence linking Pauline and the Italian couple was weak, but after she had been held in custody for a few days, she grew concerned. Then the police arrested Jojo, Hassan, and Dora. Hassan was released almost immediately, but Dora and Jojo remained in jail. "I couldn't figure out what was going on," Pauline told me. "The original investigation had nothing to do with us. But then I understood"—she snapped her finger—"just like that: Charles." Pauline had thought that Charles, who knew about only very limited aspects of her business, would be smart enough to keep his mouth shut. But under police questioning, he buckled. "They probably looked at him sideways and he wet his pants," she told me.

Charles, who had never had a criminal record and had no prior experience with speaking to cops, had lived with Pauline and had witnessed for nearly a decade how she did business. He offered everything he knew to the police, who didn't quite believe his story. But he gave them exhaustive details about the things he did know: the money trail, the names and locations of some of the crewmembers, snippets of information that he'd heard. The police weren't sure if these were the ravings of a man who was trying to pin everything on his spouse or if he was actually telling the truth. At the time, it might have been difficult for the police to imagine that a married woman would be at the helm of a drug operation in which her husband was employed as merely a minor player. Yes, women had headed up criminal gangs before, and certainly that was the case in Italy, too, but usually these women had inherited the business from dead or imprisoned husbands.

Ultimately, Charles could not give them the hard evidence that the courts needed to set him free. If he was trying to cooperate with the police to save himself, as a way to save his family—which was how Albert explained it to me—then he couldn't have known that, in addition to his race and gender, his own wife's cleverness was working against him. Pauline had transferred most of her money to the laundering operation based in London, though she still had a few accounts in Italy that she had opened with fraudulent documents. It would be enough to convict Pauline, but, as often happens with drug-smuggling cases, the full, global scope of her business went largely unnoticed.

While Charles was talking to police, they were speaking to Pauline, and she told them a very different story. When it was clear that there was enough evidence against her to keep her in prison for a few years, she told the police what they wanted to hear: Charles was the drug dealer. He was a failed university student whose African parents would have disowned him for ruining the family name, so he had stayed in Italy for years and years, pretending to work on his thesis while selling drugs to innocent Italian children. She also offered the police something that Charles could not—evidence.

"Charles had betrayed me," she said. "The whole time, all I kept thinking was that if he had kept his mouth shut, as I instructed, we would have both been out of prison. I mean, these Carabinieri, they're kids. They don't have any education. Charles could have talked them into barking like dogs if he wanted to."

She then repeated a line I had heard her use whenever she spoke of Charles: "For a smart man, Charles was very stupid." So a disgruntled Pauline told the Carabinieri where they could find his stash of drugs—not a large amount, but just enough to make it look like Charles was an average street-level dealer.

Her plan worked, of course, but perhaps too well: Both Pauline and Charles received maximum sentences.

In 1995, the year of Pauline's arrest, the Italian police had not yet come across any large African smuggling rings—in fact, not many police forces in the world had, though they knew such groups existed. Italian law enforcement was too busy with its own homegrown Mafia to even consider that there could be a criminal syndicate working right in Rome, running drugs brought from Asia and Latin America that were shipped to Africa and sold in Europe. That a woman—and a black woman, at that—could run such an operation would have been beyond their wildest fantasies. No, the police were comfortable thinking that Africans, or "Nigerians," as they dubbed nearly all black people, were only the foot soldiers, never the generals, in the drug trade. This confirmed the police's sense of how immigration worked: Migrants came to Italy impoverished and willing to do anything to survive.

To put it bluntly, the police had enough evidence—some of it real but much of it imagined—that foreigners, black Africans, North Africans, and Eastern Europeans were petty criminals. Maybe the police thought, and continue to think, that these groups worked for the "smarter" and "better" Italian organized-crime families, when in fact the true nature of global drug smuggling, which is all about seizing opportunities—markets, routes, transport, political connections—means that no one group is on top. Given its creed of making money first, the global drug trade, which is pieced together by small international groups, works far better than large cartels or crime syndicates, such as in Colombia, that grow, produce, and process all in the same country, because these smaller organizations have to compromise and agree on fair pricing and payment. And even the cartels have to rely on small international groups to move drugs around the world.

PAULINE SACRIFICED HER HUSBAND and her family. She left two children orphaned in the world. She did these things, and yes, she had regrets. Once, she told me, "Sometimes I think about how my life could have been. I wonder if

I would have been happy to just accept my limitations. Some-times people do that, you know. They take life as it comes—they have no demands. But to me, that was to live a small life. And since I was a child, the thought of moving from my house to my husband's being my life's single most important event, and never seeing any of the world in between, was more scary than death! I mean, someone had gone to the moon! And yet I had only ever known the two seasons of Uganda—the sun and the rain. Who would want to live and die knowing only these two things?

"You asked me once if I ever wanted to change my life, and I think you really meant to ask me if I was troubled, if what I did to the people . . . disturbed me, maybe even kept me up at night. I have thought about this for a long time. And the fact that I sleep well at night, that is what troubles me. The things I have done, that my children think I never loved them, the people I have damaged . . . all of this, and I have never had a restless night. What can I tell you? Maybe I am not of the human species."

CHAPTER 46.
A Tiny, Harmless Death

"*BUON GIORNO, BELLA!*" Marco Maccari greeted me outside on the street in front of the male prison. He smiled eagerly at me, offering to take my bag.

"Oh, no," I said, waving his hand away from my briefcase. I didn't want to be perceived as anything less than professional. "I'm fine, thank you." I tried not to notice that Maccari had a new haircut. This was our fourth time meeting at the prison since the day of the fight, less than a week ago, and I already knew that if my eyes lingered too long on his new coif, he would notice and tell me in detail where, why, and how he'd had it cut. That would then lead him into a story about how he had decided to also get his nails done. His manicure left his short, buffed, and lacquered nails glinting in the sun. I saw them as he reached for my elbow and guided me toward the entrance to the prison.

One of the things that I had always loved about Italian culture was the way people used their whole bodies as punctuation in any type of conversation. I liked the casual touching between people, the way friends of all genders embraced each other, how a kind old shopkeeper might pat you on the back as a form of greeting, or how a new acquaintance might touch your arm as she spoke to you about a movie she'd seen. I liked the idea that people were not inhibited, that they thought it okay to practice a level of intimacy that did not have to mean anything more than a simple gesture of acknowledgment of the other person's humanity.

I wasn't sure if I was imagining things or if there was something real behind it, but I didn't like for Maccari to touch me. So when he grabbed my elbow, I pulled my arm back, closer to my body. He let go for a moment and walked me over to the lockers that lined the wall next to the prison's metal detectors, but he clutched my elbow once again as we stood behind two guards loading six semiautomatic machine guns on the conveyor belt that ran alongside the entrance. I gave a little tug, but Maccari had a firm grip on my arm.

The guards gathered up the guns, bypassed the metal detector, and disappeared into the prison. I was so preoccupied with how close Maccari was standing to me that I didn't think to ask him about the guns or the guards. It was with relief that I walked through the detector on my own as Maccari waited for me on the other side.

I glanced at his face quickly. Every feature of his was angular: his nose, his jawline, even his eyes seemed sharply drawn. He wore the expression that, over the past few days, I had come to find annoying: an open stare of hunger. He wasn't starving, so there was no desperation in it—just the expectation of being fed. It was the look of a dog watching for scraps of food to fall on the floor.

I would have found Maccari downright sinister if I hadn't thought he was such a cloying buffoon, concerned only with his fine Italian suits, what he'd eaten the day before, and *la storia dell'amore,* illustrated with examples from his bygone youth. To me, he was a forty-year-old typical Italian mama's boy.

TODAY, MACCARI HAD ARRANGED for interviews with African inmates whom I had not met before. Most of the men were in for petty offenses—stolen vehicles, robbery—and one poor soul, a man of about sixty from Senegal, had no idea why he was there. It bothered me that Maccari insisted that he sit in on all my interviews, but I wasn't sure I had much of a choice about that. I was put out by his presence for many reasons, but mostly because it meant that everyone had to speak Italian, even if the inmates spoke only French or English.

Even so, I had expected Maccari to sit back and let me ask the questions, as it was, after all, my research. But instead he jumped right in with his own inquiries, each question progressively more inane and ridiculous than the first: "How do you like Italy? Do you enjoy our cuisine? What did you eat in Africa? I heard that people like to eat goat; what does it taste like?"

Meanwhile, I was trying to obtain different information: "Where are you from? When did you first arrive in Italy? How did you travel to the country? What were the circumstances of your arrest?"

It was a mess, and the inmates looked from me to Maccari with confused suspicion. As much as I wanted to storm out of the prison during those first interviews with him I tried to keep my cool. I had already called one of my professors, a woman who I considered to be a friend and trusted advisor, to complain about him. "He seems like a creep," she agreed, "but that doesn't mean you can't learn something from him. Promise me you'll stick with it for a month at least. It's research, not a party."

But my anger grew the more Maccari droned on and on, especially when I watched silently as he badgered inmates, interrupted them, or scoffed at their claims of injustice. After each interview, Maccari would produce a piece of paper, which he would ask the inmates to sign to indicate that they knew they would not be compensated for their stories. I had similar forms, but I knew their wording by heart, so I usually laid out the parameters for each new interview before anyone started talking. I found Maccari's approach, having inmates speak first and then sign a document later, coercive. The worried look of some of the men as they left the interview room made me think they feared that they had just signed a confession.

"Why don't we just stick to my forms?" I asked Maccari after our first afternoon working together. "Your document is very similar to mine."

"Yes, but you don't ask the men to sign them if they don't want to." He shook his head. "No, we need to do it this way. It protects us." I knew that the "us" he was referring to was the prison. I also knew that this was his way of record keeping, not to use the information against the inmates (although I was not 100 percent certain of that), but as a way to show his superiors that he actually did some work. He was hoping he would get some professional recognition out of it. This only added to my ire, until I finally couldn't take it anymore.

WE HAD REACHED THE end of the interview with the sixty-year-old Senegalese man, who had been brought to Rebibbia on what seemed to be a minor traffic violation. So far, the prison had held him for nearly a month while he awaited his trial. Maccari found this man's claim incredulous. "Come, now," he nearly shouted, "how can this be so? Surely you did something more." Maccari offered his suggestions: "Let me guess: You were selling drugs. No? Women? You stole something, then—am I right?"

The man just shook his head and repeated, "I was driving a car. Others on the road passed me, honking and shouting. They next thing I know, I am being brought here."

"What brought you to Italy?" I asked, trying to change the subject and regain some control.

"I came here to look for my son. He left Senegal and wrote us a letter from Rome. And then nothing." He spoke softly.

"Oh, so you came here without documents. You are without your *permesso,* is that correct? Well, how did you get the car? Maybe you were driving it for a drug dealer?" Maccari threw out each question, pelting the man with his words. I watched the man flinch and shift uncomfortably in his chair.

"Okay, that's all for today." I stood up to show that I was serious. I was done with Maccari and the men's ward. I wouldn't be back. *Damn the research,* I thought to myself. My biggest worry had been that I would not have enough material to write a dissertation when I returned to the States, but now I didn't care. I looked down at the Senegalese man in front of me and wondered why I had subjected him to this disaster with Maccari.

I leaned over the table slightly and extended my hand to the man. "*Merci,*" I said to him. "*Merci beaucoup. Bonne chance.*" It was the best I could come up with.

Maccari stood as well, with his form in his hands. He slid it under the man's nose and said, "Sign this."

The man hesitated. He stared down at the paper and then looked up at me. He was lost.

Maccari was impatient. "Sign it!"

"But where?" the man asked shyly.

"Can't you see? Right there. That line, right there." Maccari picked up the paper and pointed to the signature space aggressively. I sat down and explained to the man what he was signing.

The man picked up the pen tentatively and held it like an object of curiosity, its function vaguely familiar to him. He signed his name with a shaky "X," pressing too hard on the paper, causing the ink to bleed a little.

"Can't you write?" Maccari asked the man in a tone that was tainted with both disrespect and awe.

I stood up again, gathered my notebook, and walked toward the door.

I could hear Maccari's footsteps behind me in the corridor. I kept walking, hoping that I would reach the gate to the central part of the prison before him. I was furious.

"Wait, Asale. Wait." Maccari caught up to me. "What's wrong? We have more interviews."

I stopped and faced him. I shook my head. He looked pathetic standing before me, smoothing his hair down and straightening his suit. *This man is the biggest idiot on the planet!* I screamed internally.

Finally I said, "I have a problem. I cannot do my interviews with you. We have different"—I searched for the Italian word that I wanted, but only the weakest option came to mind—"opinions."

"But why?" he asked. "I thought it was going well. I am learning so much."

"I think we should finish for the day," I said. *And tomorrow and forever,* I wanted to say, but I didn't.

"But we have so many more interviews," he said. "Just a few more today, okay?"

"No," I said. "I will call the office, and we can make another appointment."

"Okay, as you like. I am just here to help you." He smiled, trying to reassure me. "Let me drop this in my office, and I will walk you out." He held up the manila folder that contained his blasted forms.

"It's fine," I said, just wanting to go back to my apartment. "I can go on my own. Really, it's not a problem."

"No, I insist. Please." He sounded mildly wounded. "Besides, I have that booklet about Rebibbia for you."

I didn't hide my annoyance. I sighed. "Okay, fine. The book and then I go, okay?"

I followed him through the empty prison corridors. I was glad that Maccari seemed to be heeding my request to just get the book and let me leave. Usually when he walked through the prison, especially near the exit, Maccari would stand around with all the other prison staff and talk. But today he passed them with a quick wave and we walked up the stairs together.

I had never been to Maccari's office before, and as we snaked our way down the hall, I was beginning to realize that it was at the farthest end of the building. I wasn't sure what time it was, but it must have been five o'clock, because there was no sign of life in the building except for us. By the time we reached the last corner office, I was so anxious to get out of Rebibbia and onto the bus home that I felt as if I were hopping from foot to foot. *Hurry, hurry, hurry,* I kept thinking.

Maccari opened his door and stood next to me until I walked into the large, extremely tidy room. Everything was gray, except the floor, which was black, and his desk chair, which was white and red. I stood by the door and Maccari said, "Go on, have a seat."

"No, it's okay, I'll stand here." I took one more step inside the door but didn't want to get too far away from it. I had to show him that I was serious about leaving.

"Okay," he said, and he shut the door behind me.

"You can leave the door open." My eyes followed him as he walked quickly to his desk and set his folder down. He stood there awkwardly for a moment. I expected him to move toward his bookcase to get me the booklet he'd promised me.

The way he looked at me, as if he were considering what to do next, made me feel unsafe, so I backed away toward the door. "Forget about the booklet. I'll get it later. I should just go now." I spoke slowly.

I went to the door and turned the knob. It was locked. But somehow I already knew that. I felt Maccari push my body against the door, banging my forehead into it. Panic either makes you see clearly or blinds you, and I was feeling was the latter. I could see only the gray of his suit, and it felt as if there were a thousand hands pulling at my clothes and pushing my head against the door. I heard only the sound of what used to be one of my favorite Italian words being said over and over again: "*Dai. Dai. Dai.*" Come on. Come on. Come on. I used to like this word because of the way it could be used in sarcasm, in anger, in disbelief. Plus, there was something perverse and wonderful about a word that sounded like "die." It was so simple and so guiltless—a tiny, harmless death.

Dai. Dai. I tried to push Maccari away. I kicked at thin air. My hands grabbed at nothing. I wasn't sure my mouth was making any sound. I was ineffective and drowning in a sea of gray. I was being pulled down by many rough hands. Suddenly I was at the surface again, feeling my blouse being torn away from me. The scattering buttons hit the floor like boulders. It was as if an impostor Asale was doing all the fighting, letting this happen to her, and the real me had left the building. I walked someplace into the darkness of my mind and waited for it to be over.

Then I felt skin-to-skin contact. It jarred me back to myself. I began kicking at the wall and the door. Maccari tried to pull me down farther, dragging me onto the floor. There was something sharp against my back; it was digging into me. Then there was a slight scratching sound, then a knock, then a voice outside the door.

Maccari froze.

I stumbled to get up. I grabbed the door handle and banged against it. I think I made a sound. And then I was on the other side of the door. I nearly fell at the feet of a man younger than Maccari. He stared at me, his eyes wide with terror, though for me or for him was unclear. The man stammered, obviously unsure whether he should be concerned or embarrassed. I fled quickly down the hall, trying to cover myself with my torn shirt and pressing my notebook close to my chest. I held my pants up with the other hand. I left the prison behind me in a blur.

CHAPTER 47.
The Quality of Light

IT WAS EARLY IN the morning, around seven or eight o'clock. I lay in bed and looked out the window. I couldn't see much in terms of a view from where I was, but I loved to watch the sun filter through the gauzy curtains that hung in my bedroom. The nicest part of living in Rome was the quality of the early-morning light. The sun shone in various hues of yellow, depending on the season, from a deep, rich golden color to the palest butter yellow. My small desk and computer were illuminated. They seemed to be beckoning me. But I averted my eyes, ignoring the call to work, as I had done for the last several days.

I contemplated staying in bed observing the sun's transformation as it went from morning to night. I didn't feel up to facing the streets of Rome, and I was still waiting on my permission to go back to visit the women's prison. There was no way I was going to go back to Maschile after what had happened with Maccari. I groaned thinking about it. The image of that prison staffer, his wide-eyed curiosity, the look on his face that said, *Should I be concerned or was this consensual?*—the look that said he felt like he was a victim of what he had just seen and didn't know how to respond to it.

I felt as if he were standing in my room, witnessing my folly all over again. A feeling of overwhelming embarrassment came over me. I felt stupid. I was angry with Maccari, but I reserved the biggest dose of rage for myself. I knew that I was just going to walk away from the incident, tell myself that he had only assaulted me—which was not rape—and that I therefore had no reason to fight this battle.

And it was true—after a few days, I did gloss over the memory. I downgraded the assault to a "struggle" in my mind, perhaps hoping to give myself a little more agency than I actually felt, and told no one about the incident. I surrendered. I surrendered in the way in which I always surrendered in life when something that I thought I could not control overwhelmed me. I had surrendered so much during my time in Italy that I was exhausted by it. Lying in bed, watching the sun—that was all the surrendering that I was prepared to do now.

A FEW DAYS LATER, Jojo called the house. I was surprised. He never called, and I liked it that way.

"Why are you calling, Jojo?" I asked.

"Hassan wants you to come meet us at Nino's place. Can you do that?" Nino was one of their associates. He ran a run-down coffee bar near the central station. It was as close to a hangout as these guys had, and I had been there often.

"Okay," I said. "What time?"

"Come now." Jojo never sounded like he was asking a question. It was always a command, even when he was just asking for the time.

I took my time leaving the house. I hardly went out these days anyway, and when I did, I stayed close to home. I was surprised at how good it felt to be on the streets, walking with purpose, on my way to someplace I actually had to be. When I reached Nino's, Jojo, Simona, and Hassan were sitting at a small table near the back. Hassan and Simona each had a few empty espresso cups in front of them. Jojo was drinking a beer.

Hassan saw me first and stood to kiss my cheeks in greeting. Then he looked at me with concern. "You look terrible! Are you getting enough sleep?" He fussed over me like I was a child.

"I'm fine," I told him, but I wondered for a brief moment if we could ever actually be friends.

"Yeah," Jojo said. "She has probably just been out all night with her friends." He looked from me to Simona and Hassan and laughed as if he had just told the funniest joke.

I shot Jojo a perturbed look. Hassan changed the subject by offering to get me something to drink.

After nearly forty-five minutes of banter, I asked Hassan, "So, who are you waiting for?"

"What do you mean?" He pursed his lips together tightly so that they seemed to balloon out, and then he tilted his head sideways. It was a clownish, overly dramatic gesture. It seemed like such a strange expression, coming from him.

"Well, Jojo asked me to come, and he made it seem like it was urgent, so I thought . . . " I didn't tell him what I thought—I didn't have to. Suddenly, it was clear to me that I was the person they were waiting for. No one else would be coming. I had grown accustomed to being the observer: Hassan and Jojo showed me aspects of their trade, let me tag along with them; my job was to sit back, watch, and ask few questions. I wasn't used to being the main event. I knew this couldn't be good.

I felt Simona staring at me, and I turned to her. I had the distinct impression that she was sizing me up.

"Simona has a holiday coming up, and we thought you'd like to go with her." Hassan sounded casual, as if this were a normal, rational request.

"Oh, no," I said, shaking my head. "I can't do that." My blood was rushing to my ears. I knew that "holiday" was another term for smuggling. I was supposed to become a mule.

"Now," Hassan reassured me, "it is not what you think. It's a simple trip; you call it a 'road trip' in America. Go for a week on the beach, have fun, get out of Rome. It will do you some good. Besides, Simona will want your company. Isn't that right, Simona?"

She smiled at me, but I could see that she wasn't happy with the arrangement.

"Listen, Hassan," I said, "I can't do it. I won't. This compromises my work and—" Hassan grabbed my wrist and held on to it tightly. I stopped talking.

Jojo stood up and walked out the door. Simona followed him. I watched them leave, wanting to go with them. Hassan turned my face to his. He looked me dead in the eye. He spoke softly. "This is not something you can say no to. I want you to understand that. We have been your friends. Pauline has done some very good things for you; she has opened doors to help you with your work. Now it is time for you to help us. Let's call it a favor," he said, and released my wrist.

I shook my hand out and sat back. I wanted to get as far away from him as possible. My mind was racing. What was I going to do? How was I going to get out of this? Would they let me go home? I had met female smugglers who had handlers who didn't let them out of their sight once they were told they would be taking a trip. I needed to get away from them, but how?

Hassan watched me as I absorbed the information. I hated him—really, really hated him.

"So, Pauline knows about this?" I asked, but I already knew. This was without a doubt an idea that she had either come up with or sanctioned.

Hassan looked almost sad when he said, "You are a student. I know that. I was one once. None of that will change. Really. This requires no rigor on your part. Just be you. Pauline wouldn't ask you to do this if she didn't think you could manage. She has come to think of you as a daughter. And I wouldn't ask, too, if I thought any harm would come to you in any way. We are friends, right?"

Actually, I wanted to laugh, not just at what he was saying, but at the very fact that I was in this situation. As I had done regarding all the problems of the past few weeks, I blamed myself. Albert, Mary, and my own voice of reason had warned me not to travel down this road, but I had wanted to see how far I could go, and here I was. I couldn't go much further.

I also wanted to laugh because Hassan had called us friends, when I knew that was patently untrue. He had positioned himself to become my handler. Time had obviously been cruel to him, since he had gone from being the number-two player in a profitable operation to cultivating potential drug mules. And I wanted to laugh because I knew that Pauline already had a daughter whom she had ignored and neglected.

I thought about my naiveté. For a long time, I had been eager to turn Pauline into my father—in a manner of speaking. I had been willing myself to see her cruelties as his, her character flaws as his, her charisma and charm as his. But I had to believe that my father would never have asked me to do something like this. He had given up his life as a fugitive in Canada so that he could be at my birth. Having never met my father, I took this as an indication of his love. I was certain that Isabel, Pauline's daughter, had no such examples.

My mind moved quickly. I figured that since they had asked me, they figured that I would do it. They had, in a way, cultivated me. I was sure that had been Pauline's intention all along: bring me into the fold and see if I could be trusted, and soon they would have another person, a young American girl, who could chart their drugs and their money from one place to the next. First it would be this run and then, if I didn't get caught, another, and then another, and soon they would ask me to carry something back to the United States.

I saw the whole thing play out before me. I had to surrender—there was no other way. If I kept saying no, I was not sure what would happen. They might not let me go home. They might beat me, or worse. I didn't want to take any chances. I wanted to get home. That was all I wanted. I knew I had to answer very carefully. I asked for more details. Drive to Spain with Simona. Stay for a week, drive back. I registered my doubt.

"I don't know," I said. "When would we leave?"

"Maybe tonight. Maybe tomorrow."

I felt the blood drain from me. I asked more questions. I had to keep talking, keep Hassan talking. But there was only so much that he would tell me, so I approached it from a different angle.

"Are you going to pay me?" I asked.

Hassan laughed. "Of course! This is not slave labor. We will pay you well: $5,000."

"Really? That's a lot of money." I thought about how little some of the other women in Rebibbia had been paid for doing this.

Now, Jojo and Simona were coming back into Nino's. I tried to appear relaxed. I smiled at them. I paced myself and resisted running for the door.

"How many times do you think we will be stopped?" I asked.

Simona chimed in. "There are at least two stops. If you are nervous, they will detect something. First you have to relax. Can you do that?"

I nodded.

She looked at me for a moment. "Okay," she said finally. "You are a student, so look like one. No new clothes. Just bring American T-shirts with English writing on them, but no flags or Bob Marley or music groups. No politics. Better if you have a name of an American university—do you have something like that? And no sunglasses, and not a lot of jewelry. You smile, you speak English only, you laugh when I tell you to laugh. No eye contact unless someone speaks to you, okay? You always look at me, all right?"

She paused, trying to remember if there was anything she was leaving out. "Be normal, relaxed." She shrugged.

We talked for another hour or so, until we had clearly run the subject into the ground. "Well," I said, "this may be good for my research."

Hassan offered to take me home. I had to say yes, even though I wanted to get far away from him. On the ride home, we got stuck in traffic. Hassan filled the time by telling me stories about ancient Rome that I did not pay attention to. I kept imagining what I was going to do the minute I was alone. Call the police? At first, I pictured dialing the number and having quick and efficient police come to my house and set up a sting operation, but then the image would go haywire.

I kept envisioning Hassan and Jojo coming over to the house to get me, and the police springing into action and the bullets starting to fly.

In this vision, I was shot and killed, the only casualty. What was more likely was that I would have to go down to the police station and tell my story over and over again, until I had established the burden of proof, and then maybe, if there was time, the police would catch Hassan and Jojo. I knew that would never happen. I didn't know Hassan's last name or his phone number or where he lived. And I knew from all the women I had met that once the cops had apprehended a person holding drugs, they didn't worry about the guy who was behind it all.

No. I was not going to call the police and waste precious minutes. If I was lucky enough to get away from Hassan, I knew that I would pack and get the hell out of Rome. I wanted to go back home, home, home—the United States home. I thought of Mary. I would not get the chance to say goodbye. I felt a knot forming in the center of my chest.

Hassan pulled up to the apartment. He didn't turn off the car. He didn't try to park. I tried to hide how desperate I was to get out of the car.

"So, what time are we leaving tonight?" I asked.

"I'll come pick you up in two hours." Hassan said. "Be ready, and don't overpack. You're going for a week. That's it. All you need is your bathing suit. Bring your passport."

"Okay." I said, lingering for just a moment. Two hours was hardly enough time to do anything. I opened the car door and tried not to slam it. I walked calmly to my door, my keys already in my hand. When I got inside the lobby, I darted for the stairs. There was no way I would wait for the elevator. I raced up three flights of steps and scrambled to open the door of my apartment. I ran back to my room and looked through one of my notebooks. I needed to find Albert's number. While the phone rang and rang, I started to think of plan B, but Albert answered. Finally.

"I need you to help me. Do any of your friends have a car?" I didn't wait for him to answer. "If they do, please send them over to my house. I need them to come quickly, because I don't have much time."

Albert didn't need much by way of explanation. "It's my mother, isn't it?"

"Yeah. Listen, Albert, send a friend and then have him park in front of the café in the plaza. Tell him not to get out of the car. When he gets here, have him call me, or you call me. Okay?"

I went into my room and started packing up my bags. This was not how I had wanted this to go. I grabbed all that was essential to me: letters from women I had met in Rebibbia, a few books and files, my computer, some clothes. I collected all my photos of myself, then checked and double-checked to make sure that I wasn't leaving behind any addresses or anything that might help Pauline's crew find me in the United States.

My bags were full, almost too heavy for me to carry. I looked at all the things I could not take with me: dishes that I had bought on a trip to Morocco the previous summer;

more books; a large box of newspaper clippings about crime and African immigrants from the three daily papers that I bought every day; some silk clothes that I had bought in a small town in northern Italy; research and policy reports that I had photocopied during the many afternoons I had spent in the archives at a United Nations office; more clothes and shoes that I hoped I wouldn't miss. I gathered everything that I was going to leave in a large pile and put it at the bottom of the wardrobe. I hoped I could come back for it someday.

I took a quick look around and then dragged my bags to the front door. I knocked on Connie's door. She answered not quite drunk, but getting there. She was with a British guy. I was relieved that she wasn't alone. "I have to give you a month's notice, now. Today. I have left some things in the room, but I will come back for them, maybe in a few months." I could see the confusion building on Connie's face. I knew her well enough to know that she would launch into a thousand different questions, each of which would take a hearty portion of my time to answer.

The phone rang. It was Albert.

"We are parked near the café. It's a blue Fiat; Gigi's driving. I'm on the Vespa. I will be on the sidewalk on the corner by your house. Come down. Leave your luggage by the phone booth." I looked at Connie and her friend, who were watching me from down the hall.

I spoke to the British guy; he seemed more alert than Connie. "I need your help taking these bags to the phone booth in front of the café. You know the one—it's about a half block away. And the two of you need to go to a movie or something—get out of the house. You can't stay." I looked at Connie, hoping that she would imprint the next bit of information on her brain. "Someone is going to come for me, and he may keep coming for a little while. He may call, too. Just tell him that I'm not here—that I left and that you don't know where I am. You don't know me well, you understand. We are not friends. I'm just a girl who rented a room from you."

Connie nodded her head. "Sure, sure," she said. "But where are you going?"

I hadn't thought that far ahead. "I don't know, but I will call you in a few days. Really, Connie, don't stay here tonight if you can." The British guy gathered up my bags, and Connie walked with him to the door. I followed them and handed her my keys. On the first-floor landing, I hugged her and told her that I would call her soon. Then she and her friend walked out to drop the bags. When I was certain that Connie was far enough away from the apartment, I ran down the stairs and out the front door. I felt my leg swing over the seat and I was on, trying to put a helmet on my head with one hand while holding on to Albert with the other. I was too nervous to see if we were being followed. And then I realized that Albert had gone down a street busy with traffic. He wove his way around the cars slowly and a little shakily.

When we stopped briefly at a light, I called out, "Take me to the train station." I figured I would go to Naples and then fly to New York from there. But Albert shook his head no.

He rode for a while longer, and then I saw that we were slowing down. He pulled into a pizzeria. It was crowded, noisy. His girlfriend was sitting at a table. She looked like she had been worrying. Albert sat down. I sat too. It felt strange being so casual when I feared that Hassan or Jojo would come tearing into the room at any moment.

Albert explained his plan. "Gigi is on his way here. Then we are all going to get in the car and go to the beach. Our friend has a house there; I have the keys. We are going to stay there for a couple of days while you make arrangements to get a flight out of here. We can't take you to the train station tonight—it would be too easy for them to go look for you there, and the trains move too slowly. This is safer for you. Trust me."

Albert didn't say any more. He didn't ask me to give him details. He just let me sit in silence. When Gigi had arrived safely and we were on our way to the beach house, I stared out the window at the passing scenery. "Hey, Albert," I said to him, "I am sorry for all of this. You know, I am probably being dramatic. Maybe nothing was going to happen."

Albert hushed me. "I have lived with my mother most of my life. She is not capable of not doing anything. It is not her way."

I knew he was right. And after spending nearly every day in the prison with women who had been betrayed by some of the closest people to them, I knew that I had to act, and act swiftly.

Still, maybe I had asked too hastily, too dramatically. Pauline might not have sent Hassan and Jojo looking for me. Maybe they had shown up at my apartment and, not finding me, left peacefully. Maybe. And maybe, if I had just stayed behind, they would never have shown up at my apartment at all. But that was not a risk I was willing to take.

Epilogue: Straitjackets

THAT MARY'S LETTER MANAGED to reach me almost ten months to the day after our last visit was a triumph of the U.S. postal service. It had been mailed to an old address of mine in Manhattan and then forwarded twice, first to an old address in Brooklyn and then to my new apartment. It was late summer when it finally arrived.

When I saw the envelope sitting in the mailbox, with its stamps of the etchings of the Rocca di Urbisaglia, a castle in Marche, Italy, and saw the "Ms." that Mary always put in front of my name and hers, I grabbed the letter eagerly and raced up the stairs to read in peace.

I tore the letter open, but then hesitated before I unfolded its pages. Mary had vanished from my life, but then again, I had also vanished from hers. When I returned to the United

States from Italy after two weeks of hiding out at Roberto's beach house, I had moved around New York like a fugitive. I wasn't sure why, but it felt safer to slink around the city, covering my tracks, and trying to go unnoticed. I felt there was little danger that Pauline would track me back to the States. She had never done business here, as far as I knew, but she did have connections in Colombia and Brazil. How far she might go to make me pay for skipping town was not something I was willing to treat casually.

I GOT TIRED OF looking over my shoulder, but I didn't stop until I heard from Albert, who performed an act of great generosity for me: A month after I left he broke his silence and went to see his mother to speak to her on my behalf. In an email, he told me, "Of course, at first she denied knowing anything about your trouble with Hassan. I didn't believe her and told her as much. She stuck with her story. You know her; she is stubborn. I asked her to leave you alone. I told her that we were friends and that I was the one who got you out of Rome. Man, she was angry about that!"

Albert promised her that he would keep in touch and even visit her from time to time. I felt grateful to him, thinking that maybe Pauline would give me some of the credit for a renewed lifeline to her son. Pauline may not have been the world's best mother, but she loved Albert as deeply as she could—he knew this. She accepted his offer enthusiastically. I am sure she wanted nothing more than to be in his good

graces. No doubt she envisioned him coming back to Rebibbia on a weekly basis. But Albert had failed to mention to her
that he was going to go to Uganda for a time, and then had
plans to move to London with his girlfriend. He was making
his escape. He explained, "I want a new start. I want to be
someplace where I can pretend that I belong."

Albert wrote me only one other time, after he moved to
London. His email was light on details, but he told me that his
sister, Isabel, was living with him and that he had been thinking about getting married.

THE LETTER FROM MARY was not the first news I'd received from Italy since my departure. After I received Albert's
first email, I took a chance and started writing to a number of
prisoners at Rebibbia. I heard from other women, and even
from a few men, but never from Mary during those early
months. But I persisted. I wrote her nearly every week. It was
almost as if I had continued exactly where I had left off before leaving Rome. But after a couple of months, I gave up
hope. Yet now, something that she had held in her hands was
in mine, in my living room in the States. It was simultaneously
a relief and nerve-racking.

My eyes fell on the return address on the envelope that
lay next to me. Via Bartolo Longo 92. Mary was still imprisoned in Rebibbia. I wasn't sure that I wanted to know what
had kept her from contacting me for so long. Had she been
punished for all these months for supposedly having drugs? Or

had she simply decided that she needed to create some distance between the two of us, given her tension with Pauline? And had my abrupt leaving and act of "betrayal" against Pauline made it worse for Mary?

I pulled the thin piece of paper from the envelope and tried to fight back my unhappiness. The letter was one single-sided note. It was hardly enough to answer all the questions that I had for her.

Dearly Sis,

How are you fairing over there? I am very worried about you because this is the very first time I've noticed you sound desperate in our mails. Well, I got a job! I have been working outside for a family as their housemaid, just an opportunity to be outside. I leave Rebibbia at 6:30 AM and come back at 11:00 PM. Plus I still work in the prison. I know that they are using me but what can I do? I still have five months or so to go here but I am dead tired. I cannot push on anymore here. Anything to take me out of this place I am willing to do. Don't worry about me. Really, I am fine, doing my very best. Thanks for everything honestly, I appreciate it. When you are replying to this letter please put your phone number so that I'll phone you often. I have the opportunity to phone you now as I am outside almost all the hours of the day.

*God bless and please try and worry less and take
good care of yourself.*

*Love,
Mary J.*

Three days later, I was surprised with another letter from
Mary. Like the first note, this letter also seemed to pick up in the
middle of a conversation. I looked for a date. There wasn't any,
which was strange, as Mary was meticulous about those sorts of
things. I looked at the envelope: December 1997. The letter I
had received a few days ago had been written seven months after
this one. But this envelope was heavier than the first, so I looked
forward to what Mary used to call a "hearty letter." But when I
opened it, it was clear that she had not received any of mine.

Dearly,

*How are you fairing over there? Is there something
wrong? I have not heard from you. I am very concerned because I have had no mail from you since
the two letters on the 8th and then on the 9th evening, almost three weeks ago! I pray everyday for
you, my dearest friend. I pray to God that nothing
bad has come to pass.*

*I am working outside with the Italian family. I
want you to know that everything is fine except that
there is so much housework to do in said family. I work*

more than I could believe, there is no time for a break. It's typical slavery and profiting off a person, but as you know friend, I have no other choice, so I do it. Here it is not easy for blacks to have anything but housework not to talk of somebody from prison! I pray someday that God will help me out of these pains. Okay, stop being sad about me, laugh it off, it will pass.

I think I will be finishing this whole thing by the first of February. Then I will be free forever. No matter what, I will always communicate with you so you will know what I am doing at any point in my life, always. You have been a good friend, a friend God found for me in my time of hardship here in this place. I can never forget you. How can I? You know how the world looks at people from prison, but you never looked at me like that neither have you judged my mistakes. I don't have much to say today because I am still incarcerated but someday, I will be free and then we will be able to laugh and talk as true friends do.

It's funny though to believe that I think of you like somebody I've known my whole life. Always know that you are in my thoughts no matter where I am or what I am doing. Please write when you receive this letter. God bless you, my friend and sister.

Love,
Mary

Mary's letter moved me into action. I wrote almost daily, and when I was too busy to write, I sent postcards, sometimes two or more on the same day. When I got no reply, I asked other women I wrote to at Rebibbia to pass messages on to Mary. I operated out of urgency, fear; I hated the thought that she, who had waited for years to hear from her own children, would have to wait for a letter from me. With the exception of the one threatening letter she had gotten from Eddie, I was the only person who ever wrote to her. I didn't want to let her down.

Still, weeks went by and I received no reply—not even a lost letter from Mary found its way to me. But if I had been paying attention instead of fretting about her, I would have noticed that all my letters from people detained in Rebibbia were slow to arrive. And suddenly, they stopped altogether. One day I came home to a bundle of envelopes. Someone at the post office had taken the time to neatly stack and bind them with crisscrossing rubber bands. There was no mystery in who had sent them—I saw my name in the upper left corner. On every envelope was a dark, heavy line running through the intended recipient's name: Mary, Christina, Folake, Bena, Grace—all of my letters to them had been sent back to me.

I checked the time. I wanted to call the prison and find out what was going on. And if they wouldn't answer my questions, I told myself, I would phone the minister of justice. But it was after 7:00 PM in Rome. I would have to wait until morning. I hardly slept that night as I planned my conversation in Italian in my head, working out the best way to sound natural and authoritative. I needed answers, but I wasn't confident that I would get them.

THE NEXT MORNING, I sat on the floor of my apartment, my notepad in front of me and the phone at my side. I was prepared for a full day of hunting down information; I knew from my experience in Rome what it was like to have to phone Rebibbia. They would keep me waiting, pass me around to various unhelpful people who would shout into the phone, "No. What it is that you want? Who? No, not this office, call this number! What? I don't understand, hang on!"

And then I would hear the echoes of leather-soled shoes slapping against a concrete floor, until, presumably, they were out the door and down the hall. If I was lucky and someone would actually return to the phone, five or maybe ten minutes later, I would be instructed to call back at a certain time to speak to a person who could help me. Of course, when I did call back, either the phone would ring and ring and no one would answer, or the same exasperated staff person would tell me that the individual I needed to speak to was out and I should call back tomorrow.

Apparently, calling the prison from New York was no different from calling it from Italy. After forty-five minutes of getting nowhere, I rang the office of the minister of justice. They bumped me around a bit, until finally a man got on the phone.

"Yes?" He sounded distracted.

"Listen, I am a researcher who was working in Rebibbia Femminile with foreign inmates, and now it seems that I cannot contact any of them—"

He interrupted me. "Ah, yes, we had them transferred."

"Transferred? But where?" I was confused. How could they have transferred all of these women without my knowing somehow? It seemed strange.

"Civitavecchia," he said.

"All of them?" I still couldn't believe it. "Can I get the address for the prison?"

"Yes, all of them, and no, I don't have the address of the prison. Call back later; maybe someone can help you." He hung up the phone.

I would never know if the man was telling me the truth about all of the foreign women in Rebibbia being transferred, but I kept writing. I even sent a note to Pauline but, not surprisingly, got no reply. I reluctantly faced the possibility that Mary and Pauline and all the other women I had met had indeed been transferred and were now out of my reach. Perhaps because I had written to them at Rebibbia, prison officials were under no obligation to forward my letters on to them at Civitavecchia.

Mary's release date of February 1, 1998, came and went, but I never heard from her again. I had nothing to point me toward where she might be, besides a single conversation we had had nearly three years earlier.

I had always imagined Mary's leaving Italy at the first opportunity, to return to Nigeria and get her sons. I envisioned her heroically making the dangerous trek back into Liberia, a country that was at war until August 2003. But when we spoke that day in Rebibbia, Mary showed me that poignant, tidy endings happened only in films.

"When I leave this place," she said that afternoon, "I am going to head north—go anywhere but Italy—and find myself a job."

"You won't go back to Nigeria?" I asked, shocked at her revelation.

She laughed. "And do what? The people that have my sons, *if* they still have them, will not give them to me for free. If I went back there or back to Liberia, what good do I bring my children? Eddie will only make me work for him, and I will not return to any prison, not in Europe and not in Africa. And I have no country. So I will stay in Europe, work and save money for my children." She watched my face for my reaction.

"Don't look so disappointed!" she admonished me with a slight smile. "You know my choices are no choices at all. When a person lives like this, looking at one straitjacket or another, we only get to determine the size, not the color.

We can only hope to get a jacket that gives us a bit of room and a hint of dignity so that we can survive."

Author's Note

THERE HAVE BEEN MANY years between the research that took me inside the prison and the writing of this book. In Rebibbia, I interviewed nearly forty women from all over Africa about their incarceration. I also spoke to thirty-two men and women about the roles they played in the international drug trade. While I was in Italy, I also had the privilege of using the archives at the United Nations Interregional Crime and Justice Research Institute in Rome.

I relied heavily on the memories of the people who were present at the time the events depicted in this book occurred. I was able to confirm most of their experiences and conversations through interviews with witnesses and collaborators. In many cases, I was able to verify the locations, dates, or times of particular events through secondary sources and through visits to some of the places described to me.

There are no composite characters in this book. I chose not to change the name of Mary Johnson; I only distanced the kinship ties between her and Prince Johnson, currently a senator of Nimba Country, Liberia, as Mary asked me to when we met in 1996. Other than that, I have not altered any other facts or features of her story.

I have used a pseudonym for the woman called Pauline Zeno and for the man I call Hassan. Out of respect for Pauline's family members—especially Albert, who showed me so much kindness—I have changed their names. Aside from this, I have not changed any other aspect of Pauline's story. Likewise, I have changed the names of the prison staff, except for the wardens. The professional titles of the prison staff have not been changed.

I had written about Mary Johnson before but, perhaps out of an excess of caution, had avoided the story of "Pauline." When I began teaching and writing about globalization and African women, I returned to the research that I had done on drug smuggling and spent several more years reading about everything from the "war on drugs" in the United States to the complex feuds between rival cartels in Colombia. But I always returned to trafficking in and out of Africa. What I have observed over the past decade is the sheer persistence of drug smuggling in that region. Even as the use and market prices of cocaine and heroin fall, Africa, and West Africa in particular, has been a resilient and almost unchallenged gateway.

While reporting on this issue of African drug smuggling has been sparse, Antonio Maria Costa, executive director of the

United Nations Office on Drugs and Crime (UNDC), has for years now been warning governments of this growing problem.

There is the threat that some West African countries could become what the UNDC calls "another Mexico." Not long ago, Mexico was a transit country for cocaine being run out of Colombia. Eventually, after years of being "service providers" to large cartels, Mexican groups took control of the traffic of drugs from Latin America into the United States.

Like Mexico, West Africa, particularly Nigeria, has a long history and close relationships with Latin American drug cartels. The fear is that with the mounting strain of poor economies and weak governments, West African nations like Guinea-Bissau, which has been called Africa's "narco-state" in the press, could, like Mexico, succumb to the same kind of open warfare between the state and criminal gangs. And given the overall fragile stability in the region, with the recent histories of conflict in places like Sierra Leone, Liberia, and the Ivory Coast, and sectarian violence in Nigeria, the concern is that if countries fall to narco-traffickers, they could bring neighboring countries down with them. We already see the early signs of drug smuggling bleeding across borders in places like Guinea-Bissau and Guinea, as well as Nigeria, Benin, and Togo.

There are many ways to write a book about drug smuggling. There are many good books and articles that provide details about various aspects of trafficking, from smuggling routes to how and where money flows. But it is rare to find material that discusses the extensive involvement of women in this trade. I chose a narrative account because of the teacher in me. My former students at the University of Texas and at New York University showed me that the books they were most drawn to and most affected by were the ones that offered intimate portraits of individual lives. There is nothing too strange or too impossible to imagine when a person gets a brief glimpse into someone else's life and touches a small piece of her humanity. For the sake of Mary and Pauline, I hope I have been able to do just a little bit of that.

Acknowledgments

I OWE MY GRATITUDE TO the many African women I met while I was at Rebibbia. Their stories don't appear in these pages, but the friendships that I made while I was there enriched my life personally and professionally. I also extend my thanks to the men who were imprisoned in Nuovo Complesso for sharing their stories.

Of course, without permission from the Ministero della Giustizia (formerly the Ministero di Grazia e Giustizia) to enter those facilities, telling this story would have been impossible.

Stefano Liberti helped me in countless ways, especially in the early days of my life in Rome. I am happily indebted to him and his wonderful mother, Cristina Liberti.

The making of this book has been long and varied. Over the years, many of my friends and former students have supported me with tremendous kindness, wisdom, and humor. To all of my friends, thank you. A special thanks to Alycia

Smith-Howard Timmis and Mark Timmis. Douglas Diaz has been with this project since its infancy and has moved boxes, given me technical support, and answered urgent late-night phone calls more times than either of us cares to remember. The diversions he provided and the rousing games of gin rummy I played with him and David Clifford when they came to visit me in Rome are what gave me some of my best memoriesof Italy.

Many thanks to Seal Press for taking on the book; the support of my editors, Brooke Warner and Annie Tucker, has been immeasurable. I am grateful to Annie for her patience and keen eye.

IT WAS AN EARLY conversation with Clive Priddle that gave this project a narrative structure. His suggestions were absolutely invaluable.

Without my intrepid agent, Ayesha Pande, this book would still be a proposal. My appreciation runs deep for her meaningful engagement with this project and her nurturing of me as a writer. With Ayesha's extensive knowledge of the publishing world as both agent and former editor, she has been the perfect guide to get me through the rough terrain.

I am profoundly grateful to the people who surround me with love every day of their lives. Knowing that my sister, Lira Angel, was on hand to offer words of encouragement and much-needed recollections of our childhood made the difficult and lonely moments of writing all the more bearable.

My lovely sons have been patient and understanding as I locked myself away for more hours than I wanted to in order to hand in the manuscript on time. I am so very thankful to them for always teaching me what is meaningful about life.

Anita Bingcang and Milagros (Mila) Soriano cared tenderly for my children while I worked. I am very lucky to know them. To say thank you is hardly adequate, but thank you both nonetheless.

Mary Johnson befriended me, taught me, and tried to protect me during my research. Without her, I would not have dreamed of writing this book.

Alan J. Hanson has been honest and inspiring and loving every step of the way. I could not have written this without his generosity, his integrity, and his insights. By example and with love, he shows me every day what is possible.

About the Author

ASALE ANGEL-AJANI earned her MA and her PhD in anthropology from Stanford University. She is the author of numerous articles and is the coeditor of the collection *Engaged Observer.* Angel-Ajani has traveled from West Africa to South America witnessing the impact of drug trafficking and civil war on the lives of women. Before turning to writing full-time, she was a professor at New York University and the University of Texas at Austin. She is married and has two young children. This is her first book.

Selected Titles From Seal Press

For more than thirty years, Seal Press has published
groundbreaking books. By women. For women.

Voices of Resistance: Muslim Women on War, Faith, and Sexuality, edited by
Sarah Husain. $16.95, 978-1-58005-181-1. A collection of essays and poetry on
war, faith, suicide bombing, and sexuality, this book reveals the anger, pride, and
pain of Muslim women.

Shout Out: Women of Color Respond to Violence, by María Ochoa and Barbara
K. Ige. $16.95, 978-1-58005-229-0. Women of color speak out on issues includ-
ing rape, murder, slavery, domestic violence, poverty, and other forms of violence
and oppression.

Women and Violence: Seal Studies, by Barrie Levy. $12.95, 978-1-58005-244-3. A
comprehensive look at the issue of violence against women that spurs the reader to
consider the impact in her life and on a global scale.

Es Cuba: Life and Love on an Illegal Island, by Lea Aschkenas. $15.95,
978-1-58005-179-8. This triumphant love story captures a beautiful and intangible
sense of sadness and admiration for the country of Cuba and for its people.

The Chelsea Whistle: A Memoir, by Michelle Tea. $15.95, 978-1-58005-239-9.
In this gritty, confessional memoir, Michelle Tea takes the reader back to the city
of her childhood: Chelsea, Massachusetts—Boston's ugly, scrappy little sister and a
place where time and hope are spent on things not getting any worse.

Homelands: Women's Journeys Across Race, Place, and Time, edited by Patricia
Justine Tumang and Jenesha de Rivera. $16.95, 978-1-58005-188-0. An insight-
ful and thoughtful collection of essays on what "homeland" means for women in
search of a deeper connection to their cultural pasts.

Find Seal Press Online
www.SealPress.com
www.Facebook.com/SealPress
Twitter: @SealPress